Stretched for Greater Glory

Also by George A. Aschenbrenner, S.J.

Quickening the Fire in Our Midst:
The Challenge of Diocesan Priestly Spirituality

STRETCHED
for
GREATER GLORY

WHAT TO EXPECT FROM THE
SPIRITUAL EXERCISES

GEORGE A. ASCHENBRENNER, S.J.

LOYOLAPRESS.

CHICAGO

LOYOLAPRESS.

3441 N. ASHLAND AVENUE
CHICAGO, ILLINOIS 60657
(800) 621-1008
WWW.LOYOLABOOKS.ORG

© 2004 The Corporation of the Roman Catholic Clergymen
All rights reserved

Scripture quotations are from the Jerusalem Bible © by Darton, Longman & Todd, Ltd., and Doubleday & Company, Inc. 1966, 1967, and 1968. Reprinted by permission.

Unless otherwise noted, excerpts for *The Spiritual Exercises* are from George E. Ganss, S.J., *The Spiritual Exercises of Saint Ignatius* (Chicago: Loyola Press, 1992).

The statue of Ignatius the Pilgrim on the front cover was created by Vicki Reid, a sculptress from St. Charles, Missouri. It welcomes all who enter the Jesuit Center for Spiritual Growth in Wernersville, Pennsylvania. As can be seen on the back cover, the eyes, decisively set on God's Love, propel the pilgrim's walking into whatever direction that Love's greater glory stretches his pilgrim heart.

Cover design by Michael Karter and Janet Risko
Interior design by Kathryn Seckman

Library of Congress Cataloging-in-Publication Data
Aschenbrenner, George A.
  Stretched for greater glory : what to expect from the Spiritual exercises / George A. Aschenbrenner.
    p. cm.
  Includes bibliographical references.
  ISBN 0-8294-2087-8
  1. Ignatius, of Loyola, Saint, 1491–1556. Exercitia spiritualia. 2. Spiritual exercises. 3. Spiritual life—Catholic Church. I. Title.
BX2179.L8A83 2004
248.3—dc22

                                                                2004014884

Printed in The United States of America
04 05 06 07 08 09 Bang 10 9 8 7 6 5 4 3 2 1

For
St. Ignatius Loyola
who led me
and all my Jesuit Brothers
to be companions at the side of JESUS;

especially for
Gilles Cusson, S.J.,
who was awakened suddenly
to the fullness of GLORY
on April 30, 2003

and

for many other Ignatian companions
who have shared their stretching
with me over many years.

CONTENTS

Acknowledgments ix

Introduction xi

1 Ignatius's Spiritual Exercises and the Word of God 1

2 Preliminary Profound Practicalities 11

3 A Glorious Foundation 35

4 A Forgiven Sinner: Awed in Gratitude 51

5 Readied for Wise Loving 65

6 A School of Discipleship 77

7 A Cosmic Confrontation 87

8 Choosing and Loving Always for God's Glory 101

9 A Compassionate Joy beyond Any Disappointment . . . 117

10 Daily Life: Gratefully Serving God in All 133

11 Methods of Praying and Some Rules 149

12 Discernment of Spirits in the Exercises 161

13 A More Probing Discernment 189

Epilogue 201

Notes 203

ACKNOWLEDGMENTS

Gratitude is the culmination of the Christian life, as this book makes clear. Thankfulness is the stretch of soul that keeps us sensitive to the inspiration of the Holy Spirit in daily life. So it is my happy task to give thanks here to the many people who made this book possible.

First of all, many years of Jesuit formation, development, and relationships have helped me to find my way to God accompanied by St. Ignatius and the Spiritual Exercises. Many years of work and sharing with the staff at the Jesuit Center for Spiritual Growth stirred the contents of this book within me. Many participants in the Jesuit Spiritual Center's Resident Staff Associate Program—often international in background—have inspired me, over twelve years, to the appreciation and formulation of the Exercises expressed here. The Jesuit community at Gonzaga High School in Washington, D.C., provided just the nonintrusive encouragement that I needed for the hard work of writing.

Many competent and kind people helped the manuscript come to its present form. I am grateful for the close reading and insightful recommendations of William Barry, S.J., John Horn, S.J., Barbara Ehrler, r.c., Maureen Conroy, R.S.M., and Dr. Michael Downey. They stretched my heart to the careful final expression of these printed pages. Geraldine Bean's secretarial eye together with Diane Ross's enthusiastic appreciation and faithful word processing gave a form to the text beyond anything I could have done myself.

My brothers, my sister, and many other friends cheered me on. But a special group of elderly friends who know the Exercises provided encouragement with prayer and concern, especially one who continues to encourage, smiling on from eternity. Jim Manney, my editorial guide, and all his helpers at Loyola Press, provided competent assistance without which this book could not finally have happened.

In conclusion, three brother Jesuits are at the center of this book. After Ignatius himself comes Gilles Cusson, who set a whole new fire in my understanding of the Exercises. Last and most of all, I am grateful to Fr. Joe Whelan, S.J., a deceased dear friend whose radiant mind and smiling heart still journey with me after many shared years in the Exercises, most especially our pilgrimage together through Cusson's book in Rome.

INTRODUCTION

The desire of the human heart is limitless. Put simply and starkly, this hunger, this longing, this yearning is for love. Love, if vague and abstract, flighty and undependable, will never satisfy. But love as an experience—intimate, personal, genuine— instills a thrill and excitement into a complacent, bored life just as the wind causes a limp, droopy sail to stretch and flex.

Without such an experience of love, disappointment drags its feet in our hearts. Life is stale. Our hearts feel numb, paralyzed, imprisoned. This condition affects us all, with no exceptions. The human heart is made for and aches for love. Nothing short of that will satisfy us. In moments of unreflective insensitivity, we do not notice, we do not even seem to feel, the dismal undertone of our lives. Frantically and frenetically, we dash from one experience to another. A whole range of distractions dissipates our hearts. In the midst of all the breathless activity, we are searching—and trying to inject thrill and excitement into life on our own.

Whether suddenly or slowly, a moment of awakening emerges: something is wrong. Like an undertow in the waves of the ocean, a sullen sadness pulls us down. As this realization grabs hold of us, a shock of fright can suck away the breath of our soul. To face such a moment, truly to enter into and listen to it, is a very risky venture. Distracting daydreams of fun and pleasure will always entice us away from the challenge of the moment. But the confrontation of this challenging realization carries within itself, often in a way hidden and furtive, a glorious opportunity laden with attractive potential. However, to run, to avoid and escape this risky, scary invitation, is to prolong the sullen undertow of life—and bypass a deeply desired enrichment.

Yes, love—true, genuine personal love—always makes a difference. It stretches, invigorates, and challenges our soul. This stretching snaps complacency, calms the undertow of sadness, and lays bare in daily life a glorious freedom. But, as mentioned in the beginning, the heart's desire is limitless. So our longing for love can never settle, finally, for the experience of some limited, finite human love. Implied in these valuable finite experiences is another love beyond all earthly imagining. The revelation of God in the beauty of the risen Jesus adds profound, inexpressible significance to all limited human loving—and lures us on in our inherent thirst for the fullness of love. Jesus himself knew that thirst for love and found it satisfied in the Beloved of his heart, that One who enriched daily life and saw him through its trials and tribulations, its joys and pleasures.

God's existence and love for each and all of us are truths on which all of reality is founded. Some people come to this belief late and after intense questioning. Others come to it early and with an apparent ease, and thus can slide into complacency. The existence of God, loving beyond all comprehension and comparison, is the most important truth about life but is never the object of cheap, easy belief. Though concepts and words have important roles to play, belief in Someone beyond the visible engages experience, graced experience, interpersonally real and intimate beyond words. This belief and interpersonal relationship with an invisible God focuses in the revelation and existence of Jesus and radiates an unimagined significance of love in all the visible details of daily life. Though our hearts yearn for a love beyond all love, belief in a God of such love is not easy, because it eludes—even defies—our control and domination. The conflicts, disappointments, and tragedies of our contemporary world provide ample evidence of what we speak of here: the heart's desire for a love that is dependable and freeing beyond any human example. It is the central issue that flames forth in everything.

The *Spiritual Exercises* of St. Ignatius of Loyola presents such an experience of God's glorious love: a love enlivening, faithful, and freeing beyond any human example. First published in 1548, the *Exercises* was born of the experience of St. Ignatius. He intended the book as a means to facilitate an experience similar to his own on the part of anyone ready and eager. No one else has ever experienced the Exercises in exactly the same way that Ignatius did. His experience is unrepeatable. But thousands and thousands of people have shared Ignatius's experience in the unique way intended for them by the Holy Spirit.

Though the *Exercises* is stamped by a number of different influences in the history of Christian spirituality,[1] the book as we have it was basically born in the experience of Ignatius during a ten-month stay at Manresa. But that Manresan experience was foreshadowed and cultivated in earlier parts of his life, especially his recuperation in the family castle at Loyola from a war wound and then a visit to the Benedictine monastery perched atop Montserrat in eastern Spain.[2] For this reason a careful understanding of the Exercises and a full-hearted experience of them is aided by an appreciation of their context in the life of Ignatius.

Central Dynamics of the Exercises

In *Stretched for Greater Glory*, I will present the experience of the Exercises by describing the developing dynamics that are at the heart of that experience. My central concern, therefore, is to detail the set of dynamics that give power and thrust to the Exercises and stretch the soul to a new identity of love. These dynamics respond to that inherent yearning, that limitless desire, in all our hearts for love, a glorious love that inserts us in the central flow of life. I will base my reflections on a full experience of the Exercises, either in the solitude of a thirty-day period[3] or in the midst of the responsibilities of daily life[4]—two approaches that Ignatius developed and described. The dynamics I describe in this book stand out more clearly in the full experience than in any valid adaptation. These dynamics are central to the Exercises. Without them the experience, however exhilarating and challenging, is not that of Ignatius's Exercises.

As we will see, the Exercises are capable of—and intended for—wide adaptation. Underlying this important adaptability, however, is a development of dynamics that determines the very essence of the experience. For all making the Exercises, these dynamics determine the experience as they stretch, purify, and shape the person's relationship with the risen Jesus for loving service. A proper appreciation of these fundamental dynamics will avoid both a mistakenly rigid adherence to the text and a misguided shifting openness, each of which misses the essence of a genuine experience of the Exercises.

To describe these dynamics is not to divulge some closely guarded secret hidden in the Exercises. Whatever secret there may be is meant to be shouted from the rooftops rather than closely guarded. The secret gloriously revealed to reverent and generous retreatants is the same as that described in the letter to the Colossians (1:27): "And the secret is simply this: Christ *in you*! Yes, Christ *in you* bringing with him the hope of all the glorious things to come."[5] As we shall see, this revelation is glory, a glory promised in Jesus, for you the retreatant, for us all, and for our whole universe.

Nor is the explication of the dynamics of the Exercises a laying out of a bony skeletal figure for study and experimentation, as in a laboratory. The product of this explanation of the dynamics is not like a cadaver in a morgue. It is, rather, a lively personal encounter, in ever greater intensity, with the risen Jesus in a love beyond all human promise. This is the love our hearts desire, and when deprived of it, we flounder, sad, perplexed, lost. These dynamics of the Exercises describe Ignatius's experience of a love that fulfills the deepest longing of all our hearts.

The *Exercises,* Ignatius's experience of God's faithful love in Jesus, is not the one and only saving way for everyone. I do not pretend such arrogance. This is the version of the Christian way to which Ignatius was led, and it has excited the hearts of many down the ages since the sixteenth century. But God's way of saving love is not limited to this version. The *Exercises* is one—and only one— of the many versions in which Christian spirituality has taken expression over the centuries.

Focus of This Book

Stretched for Greater Glory is aimed primarily at an experience of the dynamics that constitute the flow of the Exercises and is not presented simply as an academic study. Although serious study is not excluded from the book, such study loses its focus and power when separated from the actual experience. Nor is the book intended as a full commentary on the *Exercises*. Such commentaries already exist and have helped me depict the experience.[6] As a result, parts of the text will not be treated, and other parts will be briefly and summarily described.

In writing this book, I had in mind people who are interested in making the Exercises. So the book must be read in a contemplative fashion and with an open heart, thereby allowing the Holy Spirit to draw you into the experience described here. All the way through, the focus is on the reader's experience. The book's focus, therefore, is on something beyond my control: the eager desire of God in Jesus for a life of intimate, glorious love for you and for us all.

I will first situate the Exercises in the context of Ignatius's own experience and the Scriptures. Then I will give some overviews of the whole experience. In the major section of the book, I will move through the various parts of the Exercises, describing those central dynamics that unify and hold together the whole experience. Finally, I will comment briefly on the sets of rules that conclude the *Spiritual Exercises*.

Who might find this book helpful? Surely people already formed in Ignatian spirituality will read with a special background. People who direct the experience of the Exercises will find help in this description of the dynamics so central to that experience. Some people who have had the experience of the Exercises will recognize it and, perhaps, be called to renew parts of it. Other people who once had a fragmentary experience may be stirred to a more mature and full experience now. Still others who have never experienced the Exercises will learn the way of Ignatian spirituality and may find sparked in their hearts a desire for something of that experience. But the primary audience to whom this book is addressed is you who are awakened enough to desire greater meaning in life and are ready to enter anew into God's revelation. This revelation in Jesus, God's glory, will lead you into the truth of reality and will stretch your souls, in awe and zealous hope, for greater glory.

A couple of concluding cautions and a final hope are in order. First, the cautions: The book's title, while carefully and intentionally chosen, requires some comment. *Stretched for Greater Glory* can sound like a finished product. But the enterprise described here is, in itself and in your experience, clearly a work in progress. It is a work initiated, impelled, and progressing from beginning to end in the decisive currents of the Holy Spirit. And the Holy Spirit's stretching of your soul is not destructively depleting but rousingly renewing. For this reason, the book's detailed description of the Exercises can never substitute for or replace your experience as you open yourself to the Holy Spirit. May this description, rather, stir and direct your desire to make the Exercises. It is my fondest hope, finally, that the deepest longing in all our hearts can be touched here, thanks to God's personal desire for us all, a desire that surpasses all our own longing.

1

Ignatius's Spiritual Exercises and the Word of God

The *Spiritual Exercises* is a little book with an explosive potential. In this chapter I will investigate the interrelationship among the Spiritual Exercises, the experience of Ignatius, and the mystery of Christ as revealed in the Scriptures. The remainder of the chapter will briefly present five different ways of viewing the Exercises—ways that richly overlap and reinforce one another. This chapter will thus set the scene for the description in the remainder of the book of the dynamics that make up the explosive potential of the Exercises.

The Exercises and Ignatius's Experience

The *Exercises* as we have it was born in the experience of Ignatius during a ten-month stay in 1523 at Manresa, a town in eastern Spain. But that Manresan experience was foreshadowed in earlier parts of his life, especially his recuperation from a war wound in the family castle at Loyola.

The radical reorientation of Ignatius's life had explosive results, but the upheaval was quiet and unobserved for the most part, rumbling through some deeply held convictions in his own heart. A gutsy soldier unaccustomed to much introversion and whose rallying cry had been heard in many a battle, Ignatius faced a lengthy period of inactivity during his recovery from a leg wound suffered in a battle with the French. Time stared him in the face and waited on him like an unwelcome guest. With nothing else to do, he began to read and reread what was available: Ludolph of Saxony's *Life of Christ*[1] and *The Golden Legend,* a book of lives of saints. With a thoroughness, determination, and hunger for the heroic that he had brought to his military exploits, Ignatius conquered these two readings.

His reading was more than a time filler. Despite his customary attraction to fanciful, romantic subjects, he became absorbed in the religious dimension of his reading. These two books introduced him personally to Jesus Christ as never before, and his heart glowed with the possibility of a relationship so personal as to point toward a whole new way of living. This soldier's attention, usually focused outward to observe any suspicious movements of the enemy, now, in the solitary confinement of recuperation, turned inward. With a sensitivity at first not fully appreciated, but which later puzzled, amazed, and instructed him, Ignatius began to notice the glow in his own heart.

In the examples of the lives of the saints, he saw another type of heroism: he saw how far the love of God in Jesus could stretch people. An ardor stirred his own heart, a fire of desire for heroic deeds for God that would match, even top, those of the saints. All this was no less exciting than his military exploits. In fact, soldiering for Jesus seemed even more important and exciting.

During those ten months of recuperation, Ignatius knew his life had decisively shifted. A whole new dimension of inner sensitivity and personal insight, together with quiet determination, had opened for him. The pieces of his life would never fit together again the way they had for almost thirty years. Although he had much yet to learn, he was concerned about preserving what he had already gained, so he turned to a former pastime: writing. In his elegant penmanship, he began to record the passages of his reading that were moving his heart so persuasively. His great delight[2] in reading the *Life of Christ* led him to copy out three hundred pages in his own writing. Over time these ruminations and jottings gave birth to the *Spiritual Exercises*.

The book was the result of years of reflection on his experience while the radical conversion continued to have its effect on him. For about twenty years he carefully honed the wording of his experience and its implications. Ignatius knew he could not force this life-changing experience on anyone else, but he was eager to do all that he could to provide an opportunity for others. In his little book he sketched out a program that would allow others to have the same experience that had brought him into the truth and wise intimacy of a new life. The *Exercises* is surely not a simple cookbook, but it does include a recipe for an experience of God's love that never leaves a human life unchanged. It facilitates an interpersonal encounter in love that centers a person in God and generous service.

When Ignatius's little book is separated from his experience, it loses its vigor and orientation. Reduced to words on a page, it can mislead, confuse, and frustrate. In order to avoid this danger, I will often describe the dynamics of the *Exercises* in terms of Ignatius's own lived experience.

The Exercises and the Scriptures

Although Ignatius probably did not possess his own copy of the Scriptures, through his careful reading of Ludolph's *Life of Christ* he met the saving mystery of Christ.[3] So we turn now to that second important relationship: that existing between the Exercises and the mystery of Christ as revealed in the Scriptures. The phrase often used by Ignatius's contemporaries that he was "taught by God himself"[4] can be misunderstood. Though Ignatius knew that "God treated him just as a schoolmaster treats a little boy when he teaches him,"[5] this does not imply that God dictated the book to him. The *Spiritual Exercises* has no power on its own to work one's salvation. When we exaggerate the importance of the book itself, we cut it off from its saving source. Paradoxically, when the *Exercises* is given such an exaggerated importance, the dynamics lose their liveliness and take on the brittle lifelessness of a bony skeleton.

The *Exercises* does not flow in a smooth, steady style, chapter after chapter. Rather, it is "a set of materials, directives, and suggestions for the person helping another through the course. They are in that regard more like a teacher's manual than a student's textbook."[6] This manual of directives helps the one giving the Exercises to guide other people in their experience of the mystery of Christ, God's saving revelation revealed in the Scriptures.

Here in the saving mystery of Christ, and here alone, reside the explosive, transforming power and challenge that Ignatius experienced. The Holy Spirit cast a spell over him during his contemplative reading of Ludolph's *Life of Christ*. Without this radically reorienting experience of Jesus as alive, active, and inviting today, no book of directives by Ignatius would have been possible. Yes, Ignatius was taught by God, not in literal dictation by the Holy Spirit but by learning to read his own heart in a moving and challenging encounter with Jesus as God's good news of saving love.

Gilles Cusson develops this relationship between the *Exercises* and the Scriptures at great length in his book *Biblical Theology and the Spiritual Exercises*.[7] Biblical theology as the saving encounter with the mystery of Christ is the bedrock of the *Exercises*. This encounter happened to Ignatius, and it happens to all exercitants. The *Exercises* and a retreatant's subjective experience are fully dependent on the great saving deed of God in Christ Jesus; biblical theology and the objectivity of Christian revelation have the clear priority. Cusson puts it this way: "The framework, the techniques, and all the steps of various kinds which make up the book of the *Exercises* have as their only purpose the transmission, the revelation, and the realization of the salvific plan, the mystery of God in Christ."[8]

Ignatius's contemplative absorption in Ludolph's *Life of Christ* laid an extensive foundation that changed the basic structure of his life. The revelation of God in Jesus had grabbed and structured his soul as never before. At the same time, but on a different level of his soul, reading the lives of the saints quickened the heroic blood in his veins. Two contexts, therefore, are essential to any correct understanding of the Exercises: Ignatius's continuing experience from Loyola to Manresa and the saving mystery of Christ.[9]

The dynamics of the Exercises described in this book are always initiated by and intermesh with the power of God's word. At times in my description I refer to specific passages of Scripture. A lot more of this scriptural cross-referencing could have been done, since the whole retreat is a matter of prayer with the word of God. Too much of this scriptural cross-referencing, however, could distract from my central concern here: a description of the developing dynamics that form the very identity of the Exercises.

General Overviews of the Exercises

Against the backdrop already presented in this chapter, I will now briefly describe five ways of viewing an experience of the Exercises. This will provide a fundamental orientation before we look at the development of the specific dynamics of the Exercises.

First, the experience is that of the dynamic of love, or of the development worked in a human heart by God's love. An appreciation of the dynamics of human love can be a great aid to one approaching the Exercises. Human love is not a static experience but one that grows and develops, often in a quiet, unobserved manner. It must grow if it is not to die. If the parties involved take the interpersonal love seriously enough and persist in believing in it, then they will respond to the various invitations that constitute the dynamic of love. In this way a daily and continuing life of love can be fashioned.

With God's love, however, one does not initiate the encounter or plot the course of its development. Ignatius learned this for himself. Though he was a hardheaded man of practical planning and courageous execution, his experience at Loyola and especially at Manresa left him dumbstruck, awed at what was happening to him. He was so much not the instigator that it frightened him. He was being pulled beyond the depth of his accustomed control and planning. However, he learned to trust the love that was pulling him with a seriousness that based his new life on its dynamics over the years.

Second, making the Exercises is an experience of discovery of self-identity through one's encounter with God's revelation. "Who am I?" is the central question for us all. Some people are haunted by it, while others have not yet acknowledged its rumbling in their subconscious. Yet it is always there. A great variety of answers bombard you from parents, friends, enemies, chance acquaintances, and many other people. Our secular culture has its own pervasive answer, sometimes as blatant as a billboard, a television advertisement, a slick frothy newsmagazine but usually more subtle, like mist on a damp, overcast day. The result, however, is the same: a clammy dampness that does not cleanse but contaminates.

Where does one turn for self-discovery? The answer to that question can be significant in itself. In the Exercises we turn to God's revelation in a profoundly personal experience of mutual self-revelation with God in Jesus.

An appreciation of the dynamics of interpersonal encounter can facilitate the experience. How good are you at having people reveal themselves to you? How good are you at revealing yourself to others? The answer to these two questions will surely affect your encounter with God. If the Exercises are an experience of revelation and discovery of self-identity, then an awareness of one's own aching hunger for such discovery is important from the very beginning. William Peters, S.J., states the issue clearly: "The essence of the *Spiritual Exercises* is that God is at work in and with the exercitant who wants to know interiorly, taste, relish, and live the truth of his/her own being and existence."[10]

Third, the experience of the Exercises is a progressively developing dynamic, highlighted from exercise to exercise in the stipulated grace and colloquy. These two highlights of every exercise describe a movement in your own heart that not only develops in the present time of prayer but grows all through the whole retreat.

A constant refrain running through the whole of the *Exercises* is the invitation to pray for what you desire. The whole experience happens on the level of desire of the heart. Ignatius believes that desire, as the deepest, most personal experience of grace, always reveals a person's true identity and is the birthplace of commitment. In the next chapter we will see Ignatius's presumption in prenote #6 that genuine prayer moves from intellect to heart to commitment. What is deeply desired is the grace in each exercise from beginning to end.

But praying for what one deeply desires is never easy. It pushes us into a place where a serious conflict is raging for us all, a conflict sometimes not acknowledged but always crucial to our true identity. To discover what we deeply, truly desire forces us to wade into a swamp of needs, expectations, demands, casual wishes, moods, obligations, and much more. Your deepest, truest desire may coincide with one or another of these interior experiences but will always cut deeper into your heart than any of them. True desire is fire in the heart. But, rather than simply dancing on the tips of the flashing flames, it quietly burns deep in the white-hot coals. These deepest, truest desires constitute and reveal a person's core identity.

Ignatius not only counsels praying for what you deeply, truly desire, but he even dares to tell you what that is. How can he know this? A number of reflections help in answering this troubling question. Ignatius was led by God over the years to identify that profound place in his own heart where, as human beings, we meet one another and share similar desires. Though his experience is not a carbon copy of anyone else's, it touches the similarity that unites us all.

These true desires are exposed in the objective contour of the mystery of God's saving love as revealed in Christ. As his experience with Jesus stirred desires in his heart, Ignatius realized two things. First, desires sorted through and owned as true revealed his identity in Jesus. Second, this experience was not something just for himself but could serve the same purpose for many others. The descriptive terminology varies within the Christian tradition, but the reality of these profound desires is the same because they are revealed in the mystery of Christ. In summary, therefore, these deepest, truest desires are ultimately God-given, beyond any other personal influence.

For this reason, while making the Exercises, from beginning to end you must carefully monitor your desires. God is very personally present and at work in them. You must learn to trust Ignatius's stipulated desires, not just because they are his desires but because they articulate objective road signs along the pilgrimage *you* are making into the saving mystery of Christ. Finally, and most important, you must have the honesty and the patience to search your own complicated interior life, to wait for, recognize, and claim as your own the revelation of Ignatius's desires. It is as important as discovering the gold of your true self in Christ. To pray, even at times to beg, for what you deeply, truly desire can lead to becoming what you desire and will then spill over into acting what you desire. To pray for, to become, to act what you deeply desire: this is a progressively developing dynamic of self-revelation in Christ, highlighted by the grace and colloquy of each exercise.

Fourth, the Exercises create an environment and atmosphere for choice and action. Just as Ignatius learned a lot about discerning and following God's love in his life, so the Holy Spirit teaches the exercitant discernment for making and acting on choices at the level of faith. Mission, as discerned and received from God, is central to the experience because it is central to God's loving revelation in Jesus.

So making the Exercises is not simply a time of quiet prayer or a time for putting order in one's own life. Though the experience is profoundly personal, it is not narrowly individual. It is an experience with radically social and ecclesial implications. The prime mover is God—stirring, stretching, and focusing a person's soul in a unique sharing of the glorious saving mission of Jesus.

Fifth, the Exercises can be viewed as a person's own sharing in the experience of Ignatius, especially in his interior journey from Loyola to Manresa and beyond. This pilgrimage is the heart of Ignatius's conversion. At Loyola the call of Jesus Christ profoundly restructured his life. But this early change required further development and correction at Manresa, especially in his mystical experience at the Cardoner River.[11] In his reflection on the *Exercises* and the experience of Ignatius,[12] Walter Farrell, S.J., uses a very helpful image to describe this effect. The Cardoner enlightenment, he says, was like a magnet pulling into a new unity and integration the iron filings of the pieces of Ignatius's whole previous life.[13]

The lives of some saints enflamed Ignatius's adventuresome spirit, even to a selfish competition. If Francis and Dominic had done such great things for Christ, why could he not match and even surpass them? This question was like a firebrand that ignited his spirit once again. This attraction of the saints both complemented and contrasted with the new structured identity that now deeply founded his life. As a result, he stopped at Manresa after a few days at Montserrat, aflame with valor and fervor. His Manresan experience purified and trimmed the competitive excess of his fiery heroism while focusing his life even more sharply. You will go through a similar development in your experience of the Exercises.

These five overviews can be summarized by a division of interpretation about the purpose of the Exercises. Some people, often referred to as "Electionists," see the goal of the Exercises as making a wise choice of a state of life in which to serve God best. Another group, referred to as "Perfectionists," sees the goal as a union with God most intimate and total.[14] These two different interpretations are not mutually exclusive but complementary. Whether one makes the Exercises before, after, or in the actual process of making a choice of state of life, the experience aims at a fundamental reformation of life and a more faithful commitment to God with a realization of one's unique role in the mystery of Christ.[15]

The overviews presented here are not mutually exclusive but reinforce one another in a way that enriches the understanding of the Exercises at this early point in my treatment. The book and the experience of the Exercises begin with some prenotes, or introductory explanations, that prepare the one giving the Exercises and the one receiving them.[16] The next chapter will introduce and explain these prenotes.

2

Preliminary Profound
Practicalities

Where and how an experience of the Exercises begins is an important matter. The twenty prenotes and comments at the beginning of the book help us to appreciate this. They are practical annotations that Ignatius probably included as notes about what he was learning in his experience of giving the Exercises. The practicality of these prenotes is deceptive, however, because hidden behind some straightforward advice are profound implications about faith, prayer, and God's generosity.

The focus of these notes is on adaptation of the Exercises. John O'Malley, S.J., sees accommodation to the particular situation of individuals as central to the early Jesuits' way of proceeding,[1] and indeed from the first page the adaptability of the experience of making the Exercises is clear. If these prenotes are lightly passed over, one misses both the flexibility of the Exercises and profound insights into the spiritual dimension of the experience. Most of these prenotes contain advice for the one giving the Exercises, but some are also directly applicable for the retreatant. I will not make an in-depth treatment of each note, but I want to highlight the way they create a necessary attitude at the outset of the experience.

The Twenty Prenotes

1. *The First Explanation.* By the term Spiritual Exercises we mean every method of examination of conscience, meditation, contemplation, vocal or mental prayer, and other spiritual activities, such as will be mentioned later. For just as taking a walk, traveling on foot, and running are physical exercises, so is the name of spiritual exercises given to any means of preparing and disposing our soul to rid itself of all its disordered affections and then, after their removal, of seeking and finding God's will in the ordering of our life for the salvation of our soul.

The comparison between physical and spiritual exercise is helpful. Physical exercise involves stress and strain of muscle to develop and tone the body. In spiritual exercise the stress and strain is on the spirit in order to "shape up" the soul to seek and find God's will as unique for oneself.

Though it is not Ignatius's image here, the experience of sails unfurling, straining, cracking in the wind makes possible a deceptively quick glide of a sailboat. As wind stretches and increases the size of drooping sails, so these exercises of the spirit stretch your soul to a greatness that directs the glide of your life in the wind of God's loving spirit. This greatness of soul and directional glide of life are magnificent to behold but cannot be achieved on your own. They are works of God.

2. *The Second.* The person who gives to another the method and procedure for meditating or contemplating should accurately narrate the history contained in the contemplation or meditation, going over the

points with only a brief or summary explanation. For in this way the person who is contemplating, by taking this history as the authentic foundation, and by reflecting on it and reasoning about it for oneself, can thus discover something that will bring better understanding or a more personalized concept of the history—either through one's own reasoning or insofar as the understanding is enlightened by God's grace. This brings more spiritual relish and spiritual fruit than if the one giving the Exercises had lengthily explained and amplified the meaning of the history. For what fills and satisfies the soul consists, not in knowing much, but in our understanding the realities profoundly and in savoring them interiorly.

In making the Exercises you will be taught by God much more than by the one who gives the Exercises to you. The director or guide must explain a number of things, but always briefly and to the point. You will be introduced to various meditations and passages from Scripture. The art of a good director involves welcoming you into God's word and then leaving you alone with the One who wants to address you personally and uniquely. A good director neither explains at great length nor simply assigns the passage without comment but welcomes you into the mystery in a way that invites prayer. This will always involve adjusting to whatever background of familiarity with the Scriptures a retreatant may have. Scripture study is not the point; rather, a profoundly interpersonal encounter provides the time and space for seeing, tasting, and relishing the truth.

A personal assimilation of the truth being revealed requires time and focused simplicity of heart. Letting things sink into that deepest, most personal part of yourself makes this experience very different from classroom learning and much more an encounter with God in Jesus. This note, together with the following one, says much about the nature of the experience and the level within the exercitant where this experience is to happen.

> 3. *The Third.* In all the following Spiritual Exercises we use the acts of the intellect in reasoning and of the will in eliciting acts of the affections. In regard to the affective acts which spring from the will, we should note that when we are conversing with God our Lord or his saints vocally or mentally, greater reverence is demanded of us than when we are using the intellect to understand.

The experience of the Exercises is not simply a matter of intellectual understanding; rather, it is the development of an interpersonal love relationship with Jesus, always the heart of faith. Since irreverence interferes with any interpersonal encounter, Ignatius cautions us about this right from the beginning. The external expression of reverence is culturally determined and therefore always diverse. But unless external reverence, in all its diversity, is rooted in a genuine reverence of the heart, it is worthless. Reverence had become an essential element of Ignatius's own daily encounter with God. Peter Canisius, who observed him sometimes at his daily morning prayer on the roof of the Jesuit generalate in Rome, tells us: "He would stand there and take off his hat; without stirring he would fix his eyes on the heavens for a short while. Then, sinking to his knees, he would make a lowly gesture of reverence to God. After that he would sit on a bench, for his body's weakness did not permit him to do otherwise. There he was, head uncovered, tears trickling drop by drop, in such sweetness and silence, that no sob, no sigh, no noise, no movement of the body was noticed."[2]

> 4. *The Fourth.* Four Weeks are taken for the follow-
> ing Exercises, corresponding to the four parts into
> which they are divided. That is, the First Week is
> devoted to the consideration and contemplation of
> sins; the Second, to the life of Christ our Lord up
> to and including Palm Sunday; the Third, to the
> Passion of Christ our Lord; and the Fourth, to the
> Resurrection and Ascension. To this Week are
> appended the Three Methods of Praying. However,
> this does not mean that each Week must necessarily
> consist of seven or eight days. For during the First
> Week some persons happen to be slower in finding
> what they are seeking, that is, contrition, sorrow,
> and tears for their sins. Similarly, some persons
> work more diligently than others, and are more
> pushed back and forth and tested by different spir-
> its. In some cases, therefore, the Week needs to be
> shortened, and in others lengthened. This holds as
> well for all the following Weeks, while the
> retreatant is seeking what corresponds to their
> subject matter. But the Exercises ought to be com-
> pleted in thirty days, more or less.

Though this note about the parts of the Exercises seems clear and straightforward, it underlines the adaptability of the whole experi-ence as discerned in light of the grace sought and received. It also sets the length of the whole experience at thirty days, more or less.[3]

5. *The Fifth.* The persons who make the Exercises will benefit greatly by entering upon them with great spirit and generosity toward their Creator and Lord, and by offering all their desires and freedom to him so that His Divine Majesty can make use of their persons and of all they possess in whatsoever way is in accord with his most holy will.

This is one of the two most important prenotes and invites your serious prayer at the very beginning. It is obviously the fruit of Ignatius's own experience and his direction of other people.

Generosity and magnanimity are important graces at the beginning. Your own willpower cannot produce these graces. You must search your heart's desire and expose that in prayer to God. Then you must wait in patient hope for graces to be given.

The real start of the Exercises coincides with a generous abandonment of the thirty days for whatever God intends. This involves more than moving into the retreat house and emptying your bags. Oftentimes such an abandonment is born of days of pondering the cost and the risk. The "control artist," who is always fearful of letting go, must pray fervently at the beginning for this grace. To entrust yourself totally to God in the face of the month's inevitable risk of an uncontrollable and unpredictable outcome is the real beginning of the experience. But as the experience deepens, a central realization keeps the generous abandonment engaged: God's generosity toward you will *always* surpass your own.

Divine Majesty, one of Ignatius's favorite titles for God, occurs here for the first time in the *Exercises.* Clearly, it springs from the culture of chivalry and knighthood that formed Ignatius. It rings with reverence, loyalty, and generous love. George E. Ganss, S.J., says, "This title sprang spontaneously from his heart and with lapidary brevity expressed the deep reverence he habitually felt for his Creator."[4] Though this title is not familiar or endearing for most people today, I am maintaining its usage in this book because of its central importance to Ignatius. Therefore, I invite readers to try to free themselves of any contemporary prejudice and to enter the strong affective content of the term.

> 6. *The Sixth.* When the one giving the Exercises notices that the exercitant is not experiencing any spiritual motions in his or her soul, such as consolations or desolations, or is not being moved one way or another by different spirits, the director should question the retreatant much about the Exercises: Whether he or she is making them at the appointed times, how they are being made, and whether the Additional Directives are being diligently observed. The director should ask about each of these items in particular. Consolation and desolation are treated in [316–324], the Additional Directives in [73–90].

One of the most frustrating experiences for the director of the Exercises is a retreatant's report that "nothing is happening." Ignatius's advice here gently challenges both you and the director. If you are truly engaged in prayer, he expects something to happen; he presumes a movement from thinking the material over, to personal prayer of your heart, and, finally, to your personal commitment. So if nothing *seems* to be happening, Ignatius invites the director to investigate the details of your involvement in the practice of prayer.

This is not a matter of a director's distrusting your report but an invitation to believe in God's faithful presence whenever you come to prayer. The "nothing happening" experience can sometimes be a symptom of a deeper resistance stirring beneath your consciousness, seeking the light of God's saving love. If God is always present, then when we engage that presence in faith, *something* is "happening." This quiet presence in faith is a prayer lesson that most people entering the Exercises must learn.

> 7. *The Seventh.* If the giver of the Exercises sees that the one making them is experiencing desolation and temptation, he or she should not treat the retreatant severely or harshly, but gently and kindly. The director should encourage and strengthen the exercitant for the future, unmask the deceptive tactics of the enemy of our human nature, and help the retreatant to prepare and dispose himself or herself for the consolation which will come.

Your director in this experience is a companion in faith and offers support accordingly. In a time of desolation and temptation, which can strangle the joy and obvious effectiveness of prayer, the director is gently and kindly encouraging. This involves much more than an embrace or a pat on the back (though these have their place at times). To help you recognize the temptations of the enemy of our human nature[5] and to remind you that consolation is sure to return are the most profound and faith-filled forms of encouragement for one involved in the battle of the inner spirits.

8. *The Eighth.* According to the need perceived in the exercitant with respect to the desolations and deceptive tactics of the enemy, and also the consolations, the giver of the Exercises may explain to the retreatant the rules of the First and Second Weeks for recognizing the different kinds of spirits in [313–327 and 328–336].

9. *The Ninth.* This point should be noticed. When an exercitant spiritually inexperienced is going through the First Week of the Exercises, he or she may be tempted grossly and openly, for example, by being shown obstacles to going forward in the service of God our Lord, in the form of hardships, shame, fear about worldly honor, and the like. In such a case the one giving the Exercises should not explain to this retreatant the rules on different kinds of spirits for the Second Week. For to the same extent that the rules of the First Week will help him or her, those of the Second Week will be harmful. They are too subtle and advanced for such a one to understand.

10. *The Tenth.* When the one giving the Exercises perceives that the retreatant is being assailed and tempted under the appearance of good, the proper time has come to explain to the retreatant the rules of the Second Week mentioned just above. For ordinarily the enemy of human nature tempts under the appearance of good more often when a

person is performing the Exercises in the illuminative life, which corresponds to the Exercises of the
Second Week, than in the purgative life, which corresponds to those of the First Week.

These notes reveal that the experience is centrally concerned
with discernment of spirits—the sensitive, faith-filled sorting out of
spontaneous moods, impulses, and urges in order to see which are
from God and which are not. Ignatius was intensely engaged on
this curve of learning all through his time at Loyola and Manresa.
As attested in his *Autobiography,* this "experience of the different
spirits from the lessons he had received from God" provided guidance all along the rest of his pilgrim life.[6]

The two separate sections of guidelines about discernment
have different concerns and are to be applied to you only when
your experience demonstrates the need of one section or the other.
The first section deals with gross and open temptations, whereas
the second section treats temptation under the appearance of
good. These rules are not studied for their own sake. They are
properly learned from God when they serve as helpful commentary and explanation for the experience you are having. This
subtle art of discernment can be misleading unless properly
applied by the director; to misapply the remedies of these two sections may cause confusion and harm. In the closing chapters of this
book I will comment on these two sets of discernment rules.

11. *The Eleventh.* It is helpful for a person receiving the Exercises of the First Week to know nothing about what is to be done in the Second, but to
work diligently during the First Week at obtaining
what he or she is seeking, just as if there were no

anticipation of finding anything good in the Second.

This seems very practical and clear: do not run ahead of yourself in the experience. But this is more than just a caution against "reading ahead"; hidden in this practical advice is the essential value of a directed retreat experience. By letting your attention be focused ever more fully and trustingly in the present moment, you are developing a God-centered sensitivity. So often a person's psychic energy is siphoned off by difficult memories of the past or by worrisome concern about the future. To live carefully attuned to the *now* of the present moment allows you to find and live an intimacy with God's love in what is always its only real presence.

12. *The Twelfth.* The one giving the Exercises should insist strongly with the person making them that he or she should remain for a full hour in each of the five Exercises or contemplations which will be made each day; and further, that the recipient should make sure always to have the satisfaction of knowing that a full hour was spent on the exercise—indeed, more rather than less. For the enemy usually exerts special efforts to get a person to shorten the hour of contemplation, meditation, or prayer.

Here again discernment is the heart of the matter. The faith and prayer of human beings must always be incarnated in time. How long you pray should not simply be the result of some spurt of emotion or casual happenstance. A set length that you know you are capable of should be determined for each of the four or five daily periods of prayer. To regularize this set length invites you beyond the superficial and fluctuating measure of "praying as long as you feel like it" and into the deeper interpersonal dimension of faith.

The issue, then, becomes one carefully discerned in faith. Consciously to offer the determined length of time as your gift to God will raise the question of why you would stop early and withdraw the gift offered. Sometimes it is better at first not to schedule your generosity beyond what is appropriate to you. A sixty-minute period is not endowed with any magical value. To start with the graced length of prayer you are being given provides leeway for the Holy Spirit to stretch your generosity and the length of time of each prayer period.

> 13. *The Thirteenth.* This too should be noted. In time of consolation it is easy and scarcely taxing to remain in contemplation for a full hour, but during desolation it is very hard to fill out the time. Hence, to act against the desolation and overcome the temptations, the exercitant ought to remain always a little longer than the full hour, and in this way become accustomed not merely to resist the enemy but even to defeat him.

At first glance this advice can seem tinged with the Pelagian error that we can attain knowledge of God through our own efforts. When the prayer is not going well, pray longer. When you feel like stopping early, continue even longer. It sounds like spirituality by your strength with a teeth-gritted compulsiveness.

Rather, the issue here is profoundly one of discernment. Consolation and desolation are faith interpretations of the movements of your heart. This is the scenario within which decisions about prayer (even such an apparently slight matter as length) should be made. In consolation, the Holy Spirit is primarily at work absorbing you into the contemplation; whereas in desolation, the enemy of our human nature, that evil spirit opposed to God's Holy Spirit, is distracting you with temptations or inducing a sluggishness of spirit. In the face of desolation what is needed is faith's honest interpretation and courageous response. This is what Ignatius wants you to realize in the very beginning of the experience. Something much more than compulsiveness and Pelagian self-determination is at issue here.

> 14. *The Fourteenth.* If the one giving the Exercises sees that the exercitant is proceeding with consolation and great fervor, he or she should warn the person not to make some promise or vow which is unconsidered or hasty. The more unstable the director sees the exercitant to be, the more earnest should be the forewarning and caution. For although it is altogether right for someone to advise another to enter religious life, which entails the taking of vows of obedience, poverty, and chastity; and although a good work done under a vow is more meritorious than one done without it, still one ought to bestow much thought on the strength and suitability of each person, and on the helps or hindrances one is likely to meet with in carrying out what one wishes to promise.

To run ahead of grace is not generosity but foolishness. Consolation and fervor, just the opposite of sluggishness of spirit, can rush a person to promises and decisions unwarranted in the present inspiration of the Holy Spirit. So the director is urged to caution against overly hasty decisions surging in the emotional fervor of the moment. This is not to distrust the graced fervor but to be patient for serious decisions to mature in faith.

> 15. *The Fifteenth.* The one giving the Exercises should not urge the one receiving them toward poverty or any other promise more than toward their opposites, or to one state or manner of living more than to another. Outside the Exercises it is lawful and meritorious for us to counsel those who are probably suitable for it to choose continence, virginity, religious life, and all forms of evangelical perfection. But during these Spiritual Exercises when a person is seeking God's will, it is more appropriate and far better that the Creator and Lord himself should communicate himself to the devout soul, embracing it in love and praise, and disposing it for the way which will enable the soul to serve him better in the future. Accordingly, the one giving the Exercises ought not to lean or incline in either direction but rather, while standing by like the pointer of a scale in equilibrium, to allow the Creator to deal immediately with the creature and the creature with its Creator and Lord.

Together with the fifth prenote (about generosity), this note serves as an important foundation for the whole experience. Ignatius appreciated the immediacy and directness of God's ways with each individual. In his day such intimately personal qualities of spiritual experience were overshadowed by overly formal expressions and practices of piety.

In contrast, the Exercises are not a set of paces to be gone through or a set of prayers to be said. The focus, rather, is on the experience of intimacy with your loving Creator. Your companion on the pilgrimage, the one giving you the Exercises, obviously plays an important role, but this companion must never invade the immediacy of your dealing directly with God. The presence of too many mediators makes the experience secondhand and less uniquely immediate than God desires.

This immediate contact with the Creator of the whole universe can stir an understandable fear and trembling, or it can be down-played to an apparent normality that tames the encounter. For this reason, an important step at the beginning of the experience is to place yourself in prayer before the Creator's loving promise of such immediate communication. Such promised immediacy is humbling and even fearsome. So it takes time to welcome and to enter into such intimate mutual communication.

It is interesting to learn that this fifteenth prenote was the part of the *Exercises* most challenged and attacked by critics of Ignatius. An Illuminist heresy was raging in sixteenth-century Spain when Ignatius was proposing immediacy of communication with God. Most Illuminists, by exaggerating the directness of illumination, ended with a mystical subjectivism. They denied any ecclesial guidelines and settled for an utterly spontaneous immediate encounter beyond any norms, under the influence of what they called the Holy Spirit. Accusations of this heresy sat Ignatius in a prison cell a few times and helped to clarify his own view.[7]

Ignatius learned from this criticism; he knew he needed more formal study of philosophy and theology as a foundation for sharing his experience of spiritual development. But he would not dilute the importance of immediacy of contact with the loving Creator. He remembered well his reading and praying at Loyola, where the immediacy of God's presence, at first not recognized, seared his soul and roused the desires of his heart. The embrace of love and praise of the Creator and Lord continued to be intimately present, disposing his soul for what was God's uniquely intended greater service. The directness and immediacy of the Creator's embrace was at the heart of his daily life.

This intimately immediate communication is the most challenging and, at the same time, the most fulfilling aspect of the Exercises. This encounter requires preparation. Serious reflection and reverent prayer by you as retreatant and by your director about the Holy Spirit's promised immediacy of communication will bring enlightenment and encouragement regarding your respective roles in this encounter.

> 16. *The Sixteenth.* For this purpose—namely, that the Creator and Lord may with greater certainty be the one working in his creature—if by chance the exercitant feels an affection or inclination to something in a disordered way, it is profitable for that person to strive with all possible effort to come over to the opposite of that to which he or she is wrongly attached. Thus, if someone is inclined to pursue and hold on to an office or benefice, not for the honor and glory of God our Lord or for the spiritual welfare of souls, but rather for one's own temporal advantages and interests, one should try to bring oneself to desire the opposite. One should

make earnest prayers and other spiritual exercises
and ask God our Lord for the contrary; that is, to
have no desire for this office or benefice or anything else unless the Divine Majesty has put
proper order into those desires, and has by this
means so changed one's earlier attachment that
one's motive in desiring or holding on to one thing
rather than another will now be only the service,
honor, and glory of the Divine Majesty.

The Exercises aim at rousing and owning the truest, deepest
desires of your heart. As the previous prenote reminded you, this
is God's work—but it does require your cooperation with God's
grace. In his own conversion Ignatius learned how strong and disordered some attachments of his heart could be. Here he shares
the fruit of his own experience.

When you come upon a strong, disordered attachment—an
excessive eagerness to be admired and famous for your own sake,
for example—it can be freeing to pray against that attachment
by praying not to be admired and highly esteemed. This does not
necessarily mean that you will never be admired again; but the
nerve of the prideful sting is cut, and whatever fame and esteem
come will be for God's glory and not your own. This is a bit of
spiritual psychology that Ignatius shares as the experience begins.

17. *The Seventeenth.* It is very advantageous that
the one who is giving the Exercises, without wish-
ing to ask about or know the exercitant's personal
thoughts or sins, should be faithfully informed
about the various agitations and thoughts which

the different spirits stir up in the retreatant. For then, in accordance with the person's greater or lesser progress, the director will be able to communicate spiritual exercises adapted to the needs of the person who is agitated in this way.

If you have never made a one-on-one retreat, you may worry about how personally revealing you must be with your director. This prenote answers and calms that anxiety. Each personal thought and sin is not the material for your regular sessions with the director. The heart of the experience is the movement of good and evil spirits in consolation and desolation. The one giving the Exercises must be "faithfully informed" about the agitation and fluctuation of these spirits.

This kind of openness is often exactly what the evil spirit opposes by counseling self-protective proprietorship in secret.[8] This is the point of Ignatius's description of the evil spirit as a false lover who is deceitful and thrives in secrecy. This kind of openness, quite different from sharing every personal thought, image, and sin, will bring peace and light to your heart.

18. *The Eighteenth.* The Spiritual Exercises should be adapted to the disposition of the persons who desire to make them, that is, to their age, education, and ability. In this way someone who is uneducated or has a weak constitution will not be given things he or she cannot well bear or profit from without fatigue.

Similarly exercitants should be given, each one, as much as they are willing to dispose themselves to receive, for their greater help and progress.

Consequently, a person who wants help to get some instruction and reach a certain level of peace of soul can be given the Particular Examen [24–31], and then the General Examen [32–43], and further, the Method of Praying, for a half hour in the morning, on the Commandments [238–243], the Capital Sins [244–245], and other such procedures [238; 246–260]. Such a person can also be encouraged to weekly confession of sins and, if possible, to reception of the Eucharist every two weeks or, if better disposed, weekly. This procedure is more appropriate for persons who are rather simple or illiterate. They should be given an explanation of each of the commandments, the seven capital sins, the precepts of the Church, the five senses, and the works of mercy.

Likewise, if the one giving the Exercises sees that the one making them is a person poorly qualified or of little natural ability from whom much fruit is not to be expected, it is preferable to give to such a one some of these light exercises until he or she has confessed, and then to give ways of examining one's conscience and a program for confession more frequently than before, that the person may preserve what has been acquired. But this should be done without going on to matters pertaining to the Election or to other Exercises beyond the First Week. This is especially the case when there are others with whom greater results can be achieved. There is not sufficient time to do everything.

The adaptability manifest in this and the next prenote is testimony to Ignatius's desire for the *Exercises* to help as many people as possible. He and his early companions had a burning desire to share with many people the peace of soul that comes from experiencing the immediacy of God's loving forgiveness in Christ Jesus.

This prenote proposes a program of "light exercises" for people whose desires are not ready for the full Exercises.[9] Such a program, made up of some elements of the First Week of the Exercises, led simple people to a consoling peace of soul born of their prayerful experience of God's loving forgiveness, often sacramentalized in confession. John O'Malley, S.J., calls this the important ministry of consolation serviced by the early Jesuits.[10] I will return to this in my treatment of the end of the First Week in chapter 4.

> 19. *The Nineteenth.* A person who is involved in public affairs or pressing occupations but educated or intelligent may take an hour and a half each day to perform the Exercises. To such a one the director can explain the end for which human beings are created. Then he or she can explain for half an hour the particular examen, then the general examen, and the method of confessing and receiving the Eucharist. For three days this exercitant should make a meditation for an hour each morning on the first, second, and third sins [45–53]; then for another three days at the same hour the meditation on the court-record of one's own sins [55–61]; then for a further three days at the same hour the meditation on the punishment corresponding to sins [65–72]. During these three

meditations the ten Additional Directives [73–90] should be given the exercitant. For the mysteries of Christ our Lord this exercitant should follow the same procedure as is explained below and at length throughout the Exercises themselves.

In his own lifetime Ignatius met people who desired to make the Exercises but could not withdraw for a full month from the responsibilities of daily life. In this prenote he presents another adaptation of the full Exercises for these people. One hour and a half of preparation, prayer, and reflection daily allows someone to be led through the whole of the Exercises over a period of four or more months. This approach is often referred to as "the Exercises in daily life."

This form of the experience has grown in popularity over recent years. As long as the essential dynamics are experienced in prayer and the challenge of daily living, this method can be as effective as that of a full thirty-day retreat and should not be viewed as "second best." In fact, because the activity of daily life is constantly part of the retreat, there is an ongoing integration and reality factor that can be advantageous. Some people are asking good questions of this early form now rediscovered: Is there a carefully discerned choice of state of life that would be better served by one or the other of these two forms? Over the four or more months, are there combinations of the two forms that are possible, such as two weekends or a six- to eight-day solitude period as part of the overall experience?

20. *The Twentieth.* A person who is more disengaged, and who desires to make all the progress possible, should be given all the Spiritual

Exercises in the same sequence in which they proceed below. Ordinarily, in making them an exercitant will achieve more progress the more he or she withdraws from all friends and acquaintances, and from all earthly concerns; for example, by moving out of one's place of residence and taking a different house or room where one can live in the greatest possible solitude, and thus be free to attend Mass and Vespers daily without fear of hindrance from acquaintances. These principal advantages flow from this seclusion, among many others.

First, by withdrawing from friends and acquaintances and likewise from various activities that are not well ordered, in order to serve and praise God our Lord, we gain much merit in the eyes of the Divine Majesty.

Second, by being secluded in this way and not having our mind divided among many matters, but by concentrating instead all our attention on one alone, namely, the service of our Creator and our own spiritual progress, we enjoy a freer use of our natural faculties for seeking diligently what we so ardently desire.

Third, the more we keep ourselves alone and secluded, the more fit do we make ourselves to approach and attain to our Creator and Lord; and the more we unite ourselves to him in this way, the more do we dispose ourselves to receive graces and gifts from his divine and supreme goodness.

This describes the experience of the Exercises in the solitude of thirty days, more or less. Notice the stress on desire: "who desires to make all the progress possible . . . what we so ardently desire." This intensity of graced desire is perhaps more focused when the distractions of daily life are excluded. But an intensity of desire is a call to and characteristic of any genuine experience of the Exercises.

Two Further Introductory Comments

After these prenotes comes a heading. It is a statement of purpose of the whole *Exercises:* "Spiritual Exercises to Overcome Oneself, and to Order One's Life, without Reaching a Decision through Some Disordered Affection." Standing alone, this heading is open to a misleading Pelagian interpretation. Today's cultural emphasis on self-sufficiency and self-determination might lead you to assume that you yourself are the subject of the *Exercises*. For this reason, this statement must be kept carefully contextualized by the major prenotes #5 and #15, where the initiative of God in ordering and disposing is much clearer. As mentioned already, you as a retreatant have serious, generous work to do in this experience, but the paramount truth can never be forgotten: the initiative is with God. As many retreatants have learned the hard way, it is possible to strive too hard and try to force one's way ahead of grace.

The accusations of Illuminist heresy that Ignatius met marked his heart. So he introduces the *Exercises* with a "Presupposition" inviting retreatant and director to "put a good interpretation" on the other person's statement rather than to condemn it. A shared open desire for the truth will unite you and the director as companions and keep you on the way to the truth.

The practicality and profundity of these prenotes provide a valuable entry into the experience of the Exercises. They give you a lot to ponder and spark serious prayer as you begin.

3

A Glorious Foundation

Having reviewed the explanatory prenotes, we might now raise the question of where an experience of the Exercises actually begins. The answer is not obvious and has often been mistaken. One could begin with the important fifth and fifteenth prenotes, which are a call to prayer in the early stages of the retreat. After that, one could read and ponder the "Principle and Foundation," which serves as a preface to the book. Or, after browsing this preface, one could seriously start at the first exercise of the First Week. None of these steps is meant to begin the experience.

Ignatius always prepared people for entering the full Exercises. He worked with Peter Faber and Jerome Nadal for almost four years before their formal entry into the experience. The Principle and Foundation served as an important part of their preparation, which was continuous with and flowed right into the experience of the full Exercises. These people did not need a few special days of preparation; they had had a few *years* of preparation.

But today the situation is different. Candidates for the Exercises are carefully selected, but they usually meet their director for the first time when they arrive for the beginning of the retreat. In this case a few preparatory days are needed to allow the revealing presence of God's love to lure you away from the busy, distracting lives you have just stepped out of. Not that this busy, distracting life is not also a place of revelation for God and therefore meant to be part of the retreat. But usually you come in a fatigued and distracted state. You yearn for God, sure enough, but you are a bit ragged in your practice of prayer and awareness of God. You need some preparation time to get in touch with your desire and thus to enter the threshold of the retreat.

These preparatory days are really an adaptation of Ignatius's counsel for you as you come to each time of prayer.[1] This practical directive of Ignatius recommends that, as you enter your prayer, you take the length of an Our Father to raise your mind and consider how God is looking at you in this instant. You realize that you are the center of God's full, loving attention. Your busy heart quiets in humility, wonder, and reverence.

In a contemporary situation this "Our Father–length" preparation stretches over a few days as you slow down, get sensitized to the desire that brought you to the Exercises, and find God's love beckoning in that desire. Scripture passages such as the following can help you to consider "how God is looking at you" at this very moment:

> Yahweh, you examine me and know me, you know if I am standing or sitting. (Ps 139:1–2)

> Oh, come to the water all you who are thirsty; though you have no money, come! . . . Pay attention, come to me; listen, and your soul will live. (Is 55:1–3)

> Because you are precious in my eyes, because you are honored and I love you. (Is 43:4)

Prayer with passages such as these over the first few days of retreat centers your consciousness and slows down the beating of your heart and even the pace of your walking. In this way the mystery of God's loving gaze stirs quiet reverence, awe, and adoration as you stand before the amazing truth: God looks on you lovingly, intently, right now.[2]

These preparatory days are already engaging you with the Principle and Foundation. This preface to the book begins with the declaration "Human beings are created"[3]—a statement bland and correct. But the Exercises do not begin with a pondering of abstract, timeworn truths. Rather, as Joseph Tetlow, S.J., says: "The elegantly spare sentences of the Principle and Foundation both express and conceal a religious experience crucial to the *Spiritual Exercises*—the experience of my intensely personal relationship with God my Creator and Lord, not only as the One who loves and cherishes and forgives me, but also and even more as the One who is at every moment making me, my life world, and my self."[4]

In chapter 1 I described the Exercises as a matter of taking the revelation of God's love very seriously. That venture begins quickly right here in this foundational preface. Four different aspects of God's love, revealed in the mystery of Christ in the Scriptures, are presented for your prayer: God's love is seen as (1) creative with an immediacy of presence, (2) moving to glory, (3) greater than any other love, and (4) uniting all human beings from the very beginning. Your prayer will integrate these four aspects into a profound foundation, not only for this experience of the Exercises but, more important, for the rest of your life. I will describe each of these aspects as you come to pray about them.

Principle and Foundation

Human beings are created to praise, reverence, and serve God our Lord, and by means of doing this to save their souls.

The other things on the face of the earth are created for the human beings, to help them in the pursuit of the end for which they are created.

From this it follows that we ought to use these things to the extent that they help us toward our end, and free ourselves from them to the extent that they hinder us from it.

To attain this it is necessary to make ourselves indifferent to all created things, in regard to everything which is left to our free will and is not forbidden. Consequently, on our own part we ought not to seek health rather than sickness, wealth rather than poverty, honor rather than dishonor, a long life rather than a short one, and so on in all other matters.

Rather, we ought to desire and choose only that which is more conducive to the end for which we are created.[5]

The Immediacy of God's Creative Love

First, as a being created by God, you are involved in a relationship with the Creator that gleams with a moment-by-moment immediacy.[6] Creation is not some fatalistic scenario within which you rudely awaken, nor your own act of self-determination, nor an ancient act that long ago began the process of being. No, creation has the immediacy of constant present tense. An awareness of this immediacy at any moment can startle your soul and excite your heart in a rush of awe even now as you read these words—and as I pen them. Being created, being enlivened breath by breath unto a final breath that lasts forever: this awareness, like electricity coursing through your person, rouses concrete desires in your heart and invites your free cocreative cooperation. Words on a page fall far short of the actual experience, whose taste and appreciation require time, inner quiet, and prayerful reflection.

The loving Creator-God, who is continually creating you in the immediacy of each moment, identifies himself to Moses from the burning bush not as "I WAS" but as "I AM." Simply to sit, stand, walk, or kneel in this throbbing awareness is not a quick, passing moment. This amazement and the prayer attendant upon it introduce you to the foundational experience of the preface of the *Exercises*—and, even more, are meant to become a style of living.[7]

Such awareness settles the soul in a state of awe and wonder that opens up a whole new vision, especially of yourself but also of all reality. The book of Wisdom (11:26) implies the answer in its own question: "And how, had you not willed it, could a thing persist, how be conserved if not called forth by you?"

The coming of Christ particularizes and fulfills this vision of being and of creation as John's prologue reminds us: "Through him all things came to be, not one thing had its being but through him. All that came to be had life in him and that life was the light of men, a light that shines in the dark, a light that darkness could not overpower" (Jn 1:3–5).

The letter to the Ephesians (1:3–4) states the reality in the apostle Paul's own way: "Blessed be God the Father of our Lord Jesus Christ, who has blessed us with all the spiritual blessings of heaven in Christ. Before the world was made, he chose us, chose us in Christ, to be holy and spotless, and to live through love in his presence."

This exciting experience of God's existential creative involvement with you becomes even more immediate when it is traced back to a moment of decision. It is God's love story of your creation and continues to this very moment and on into forever. Your conception and birth were affected by a variety of temporal elements, but in and through them resonates a decision by the Creator to love you in all your uniqueness. This divine decision, a decision of exquisite love, is truly creative. In this decision, with the help of parents, you are conceived, and the fertilized egg begins the long journey of gestation to birth. In the gaze of your Creator, you are a work of love, a love that will never be withdrawn.

Sometimes the human scenario of conception and birth does not mirror the Creator's work of love. Here learning and remembering God's love story about yourself becomes even more important. However unwanted and unwelcome a new birth may be, all creation is a story of God's love, faithful beyond any human love. To contemplate the beginning of God's love story for you in specific detail makes this experience real. Start with your birthday and count back to your conception. Listen as God shares all that was involved in that precious moment of loving into being someone who never before existed: you, in all your uniqueness and potential. What a glorious moment!

Prayer about this divine love story reveals another important side of human creation: God's creative love of you insistently invites your free, responsible cooperation. You must find the middle path between the extremes of an arrogant, unilateral creating of yourself and a shirking of responsibility before God's creative love. This is not easy. However, when you achieve this middle path, your life hums with a harmony of cocreative mutuality.

Moving to Glory

That the Creator should be so personally and constantly in touch with you is truly exciting, challenging, and astonishingly glorious. To take this for granted extracts a costly price: depersonalizing and distancing your relationship with God.

The second aspect of your foundational experience at the beginning of the Exercises is a process of the glorification of God's love. As Gilles Cusson reminds us, it is through "God's creating love" that "the universe is called from nothingness and set in motion toward God's glorification."[8] This glory is not some mental construct or a diaphanous film covering reality. It *is* reality. In the theophany to Isaiah, the words of the angels before the throne of God tell the same story: "And they cried out one to another in this way, 'Holy, holy, holy is Yahweh Sabaoth. His glory fills the whole earth'" (Is 6:3). The coming of Jesus into our universe reveals that God's mystery of loving glorification is also a paschal reality, as we are told in passages from Paul's letters to the churches at Ephesus and Colossae:

> He has let us know the mystery of his purpose, the hidden
> plan he so kindly made in Christ from the beginning to
> act upon when the times had run their course to the end:
> that he would bring everything together under Christ, as
> head, everything in the heavens and everything on earth.
> (Eph 1:9–10)

> God wanted all perfection to be found in him and all things
> to be reconciled through him and for him, everything in
> heaven and everything on earth, when he made peace by his
> death on the cross. (Col 1:19–20)

Suffering and dying as part of human existence do not deny
God's glory but are somehow swept up as part of that process of
glorification, which is resonating into the fullness of time. This
paradoxical glory in suffering and dying will be central to a later
part of the retreat. To find that glory in all is never easy, never
accomplished by hard thinking alone; but as a prayerful faith view,
it can make all the difference.

Reality in all its concreteness is the glorification of God's love, a
process initiated at the very beginning of creation in Christ and gath-
ering into the fullness of time. Wherever you are and whatever is happening to you, you are part of that enormously expansive context
resounding always with the echo "Glory, glory!" The beauty of a rose-
bud, the look of wordless admiration in the eyes of lovers, the delicate
form of a baby's tiny finger, the amber-horizoned dawning of sunrise,
the unimaginable spaciousness of our universe: all this is glory.

To stand still every once in a while, immersed in the details of a
momentary situation, and then to search for and find as best you can
the distinctive subtext of God's glory in love—this becomes an
important part of your lifestyle and keeps you more fully in touch
with the mystery of created reality. Whereas to act outside that context—to forget or, what is worse, to deny it—is to lose the big picture
and to view your daily life in a much more narrow and stifling way.

Your Unique Role

The enormity and the expansiveness of the Creator's loving glory
could leave you awed, overwhelmed, breathlessly entranced.

Though this response is understandable and an expression of grace, if it stops here, it remains incomplete because it short-circuits your own unique involvement in the expansive sweep of God's glory. This awesome expanse of glory swelling into the fullness of time is not meant simply for your admiration. Within this expanse a unique role that nobody else in the whole universe can play awaits your own discovery and engagement. In some real way the developing process of glorification depends upon your unique faith involvement. No halfhearted measure will do here. The stakes are too high: the ongoing unveiling of God's glory not only to be viewed but to be lived in the unity of us all as one human family.

This unique vocation in Christ is at the heart of the *Exercises*. The last sentence of the Foundation focuses on the importance of this unique response: "We ought to desire and choose only that which is more conducive to the end for which we are created."[9] The grace of magnanimity prevents a slipshod, vague involvement in God's process of glorious love swelling through creation. Rather, our desire should be lively and disciplined.

The word *more* (*magis* in Latin and *más* in Spanish) has long symbolized Ignatian generosity and magnanimity. However, the English word *more* runs the risk of conveying a sense of compulsive drivenness toward ever greater quantitative conquests. This *more* can light a fire of competitiveness in the eyes and heart similar to what was driving Ignatius as he left Loyola. His generosity to do even greater things for God than Francis and Dominic was contaminated by a selfish competitiveness. Although heroism was the desire of his heart, it flashed with too much of himself. As we will see, Manresa painfully purified him of much of his selfishness and centered him uniquely, totally in Jesus.

In accord with Ignatius's own experience, the better translation for *magis* in the closing sentence of this preface is "especially, specifically, uniquely." In this way the generosity of the *magis* always stretches you to the uniquely special vocation and involvement that every one of us has in the Creator's glorification through the mystery of Christ.

A Love Greater than All

At this point in the description of the Exercises, two aspects of the Foundation stretch and magnify the experience of your soul like wind filling the sails of your spirit: the intimate immediacy of God's creative, sustaining love and your own unique role of freedom and responsibility in the Creator's glorification. These two elements integrate in your experience and are as real as your breathing and the beating of your heart. The richness and profundity of this revelation cannot possibly be plumbed fully before death. Yet whatever graced experience you are now given founds and roots you, in these opening days of the Exercises, in the exhilarating excitement and peaceful centeredness of God's love.

For the experience is all about taking God's love with ever greater seriousness. In the midst of your foundational experience of the love of a God constantly creating you, this third aspect focuses on that love as incomparably beyond any other. It is a love that identifies you and thus always involves a radical shift in one's "center of gravity." From finding your identity in this world, you are invited to be identified in God, whose love surpasses anything of this world.

How is this possible? Only by experiencing a love unequaled and unsurpassed by any other. God's love not only is intensely, immediately present and gloriously triumphant but is in a class all by itself. This love is no figment of your imagination, no facile lifesaver for rescue in life's troubled waters. This love stands out as more real than anything else; your very existence, and that of everything else, depends on the truth and reality of this love.

Such a love of your Creator-God puts all else in perspective. In the growing development of your experience of this love, a moment comes when you find yourself *alone,* all alone, with God in a love that is satisfying enough, quieting the needy stirring of your heart. It transcends the squabbles about a long or short life, about riches or poverty, about being honored or dishonored. To live in that expansive love takes the sting out of those alternatives because each now is seen as an occasion for knowing God's love as fulfilling beyond measure. Even more, the insight comes: this love is worth the sacrifice of everything else. Psalm 63:3 states the dawning realization: "Your love is better than life itself." A glorious freedom springs from such an experience.

To be drawn into such an engagement of love with God spurs a certain disengagement from this world. Yet, rather than lifting you out of this world into a stance of loathing, fear, or carelessness, this experience lifts you into the heart of God's love, which is always turned in loving care toward everything of this world.

God, whose love is not identified by but, rather, far surpasses anything of this world, draws close in Jesus. This same experience of love glowed in his heart as always centered in the One he called "my dear Father." His love of this Beloved allowed him to make sense of and find love in his abandonment and death on Calvary—an abandonment and death that seem absurd and ignominious from any other perspective. The clear priority of God's love, besides expanding the soul in magnificent consolation, also strips it to a great simplicity that forestalls the idolatry of crowning anything of this world with the allure or influence of a god. In this way, as your experience of God's love expands, a glorious freedom is born. This is the true meaning of the term in the Foundation traditionally translated "indifference"—very different from a care-less lack of concern.

The tensile strength and durability of this freedom, however, always requires a careful balance among options. Among the clas-sical alternatives that Ignatius presents in the text it is not abnor-mal or wrong that your natural preference hankers after a longer, healthy, fairly rich, and honored life. The danger is either that one of the alternatives assumes such a power over you as to enslave or that its opposite seems so empty and destructive as to be a fear-some torment. True freedom can disengage you from these two potential dangers only through an experience of God's love as enough in itself. Then you realize that God's love can be known in each of the alternatives. Life in the mystery of God's love is much more a matter of "both/and" than "either/or."

To find in God's love, as Jesus did, an experience that all by itself is enough for your joy and the fundamental meaning of your life is never easy. It is not something you can manufacture but is a sheer gift to be welcomed. In the struggle and distraction of daily life, it is easy to lose the focus of such an experience of God's great love. To shrink God's love to a more manageable size is a danger that confronts us all. However, settling for a God who is too small and fits too easily into our universe is always a roadblock to the pil-grimage of finding God's love in all things.

In the quiet intimacy of that little cave in Manresa, Ignatius found a fire to enflame his social encounters there and beyond. A quiet Manresan cave in your own heart, where you are regularly all alone with God, will preserve the experience of a love beyond all others and keep focused a light of freedom in all the shadows and shades of choice in a vibrant, busy life. The fundamental dynamic here reminds you that, first, all things must be found in God's great love alone and, then, that love beckons in all things. A transcendent moment makes possible an invigorating incarnational life. To plunge into a busy incarnational life without the necessary transcendent foundation can be misleading. The most insidious results of this mistake always show up in ministry where the fire of freedom and zeal is quelled by too much selfishness.

The description in the previous pages makes it clear that the freedom of "indifference," which allows you to find God's love in sickness and health, in honor and dishonor, is not something you make but is a gift from God's distinctive, real love for you. So the heart of the Foundation is not indifference. It is God's love, a love experienced as overwhelming and as surpassing all other love. As the truth of this love grows in your experience, the indifference and radical freedom that Ignatius describes stretch your heart in eager desire.

Ignatius's terminology in the text puts the focus too much on the retreatant rather than on God, whose overarching love frees us for everything.[10] The paramount concern of the Foundation is God's magnanimous, creative love, not your struggling to forge the steel of your will into the mold of indifference. A detected lack of indifference is resolved not by wrestling yourself into the requisite position but by prayerfully exposing yourself anew to the evidence of God's intimately immediate, glorious love. The experience of the Exercises is primarily that of God at work in a glorifying love, always stirring your responsible, cocreative freedom.

A Love Uniting All Human Beings

The fourth aspect of God's love presented in the Foundation bears its own distinctive challenge. This foundational preface begins, "Human beings are created."[11] The immediacy of the Creator's moment-by-moment love does not produce a single individual, namely yourself. As a human creature, you are being created in relationship—to your Creator-God, to yourself, to all other humans, to the whole universe. In our secular culture of excessive individualism, this beginning relational identity is quickly corrupted and denied. The opening word of this preface carries the meaning of "all human beings" and clearly implies the mission of spreading the news of this communal and relational identity for us all.

The Exercises often are criticized as overly individualistic. This is surely a dangerous misapprehension to which the experience is susceptible, but the opening word of the Foundation sets the experience in an opposite direction. The book of Genesis informs us that we are intentionally created in the image of God, whose whole being is relationship in the community of the Trinity. God saw how very good this human creation was (Gn 1:31). In an overly individualistic culture, to share the goodness that God sees in the creation of human beings as essentially relational is not easy. An autonomous spirit quickly inflates ego and segregates us from one another. The very beginning of God's creating activity conflicts with this self-centered autonomous spirit, and the first word of the Foundation invites a fundamental conversion of outlook regarding yourself in relation to all other human beings.

An important question is addressed to us all: Are you ultimately the meaning of your own life? Our secular culture, with a tone of puzzled ridicule, howls the answer: "Of course I am!" An appreciation of being created in Christ radiates a different answer that spotlights the Creator's love in glorious immediacy, gifting you with life, breath by breath, right into eternity. The Exercises confront this secular autonomy all through the experience while contrasting a very different autonomy born in Christ. This contrast will become clear as I progress in describing the dynamics of the Exercises.

The communal nature of our humanity is rooted in the triune community of God, but its expression is not limited to religion, church, race, geography, or any other defining element. The community determining your relational identity is as wide as the whole human family, stretching through the whole universe. This aspect of God's creative love can also leave you breathless before the challenge and the dream that God breathed in the very beginning and then made flesh in the coming of Jesus Christ.

The Desire to Be Faithful—a Problem and Difficulty

As God's glorious vision and dream in creation stretches and magnifies your prayerful spirit, a deep and true desire flashes forth in your heart. Within the vast sweep of God's creative movement to glory throughout the whole universe, to be faithful to your own unique role assumes an importance beyond all else. Rather than haggle over why you should be needed, accepting God's call and desire of love for you becomes your overwhelming desire. It is a desire stirred in you by the Creator's intimately immediate love, alive in you at this very moment. Your prayer has brought you to this point of graced desire: to be faithful in whatever is especially and uniquely conducive to the vocation for which you are right now being created.

To feel this desire burning in your heart brings joy, hope, gratitude—but also frustration. Without having labored for it, another awareness comes at the end of this foundational prayer and revelation. Your life has not usually displayed a freedom and commitment in accord with this vision of reality and of creation.

Plenty of evidence from your past life provokes serious doubt about your future living of this new vision in the freedom of indifference. A difficulty and problem plague the desire of your heart. [12] A sour note of confusion and frustration sounds the end of your experience of praying the Foundation. While a glorious wind has snapped the sail of your soul to a new tautness of excitement and vision, a concern about whether your sail will hold and not tear to shreds puzzles your heart and tests your desire. This frustration leads you into the First Week of the Exercises, to which we will turn our attention in the next chapter.

4

A Forgiven Sinner:
Awed in Gratitude

Your experience of the Foundation leads you directly into this first part of the Exercises. The difficulty that complicated your desire to be faithful to the vision of God's glorious, creative love cannot be overlooked. It is like a fissure in the foundation and must somehow be repaired. This healing is the goal of the First Week.

Despite the spreading fissure, you must not doubt the solidity of the foundation that God's love has laid. The vision stretching your soul as a result of your prayer with the Foundation is working in you a new maturity of self-confidence, in reliance on God's immediate and creative love. An autonomy of self-power and individualism is now seen as mutiny, a betrayal of the loving Creator whose desire for you to live is even greater than your own. God has lovingly blessed you with a new vision of yourself, humbly centered on the Creator. Any unhealthy guilt from the past that caused you to be ashamed of who you are has been dispelled in a new maturity of self.

I will describe three overviews of the First Week before I enter into the specific dynamics of this part of the Exercises. This will give you a sense of the structure of this part and will keep the First

Week related to the experience of Ignatius and to the mystery of
Christ.

First Overview: Three Stages

Gilles Cusson describes three stages of this First Week experience.[1] In the first stage, fresh from the Foundation experience, you
are in touch with the immediacy of God's creative love and its
movement to glory. Your desire to learn your unique role and serve
it faithfully, though complicated by doubt, stands strong as a real,
true desire of your heart.

However, in the second stage, the difficulty at the close of the
Foundation continues to haunt your consciousness. The obvious
logic and powerful attractiveness of the Creator's vision of reality
and invitation to a freedom of indifference, while captivating your
heart, have not shaped the path of your past life. What makes clear,
compelling sense, you have not done. This incongruity taunts your
heart while it begs for an explanation. Pursuing this explanation
will lead you into the depths of the mystery of evil and sin. You will
share the helplessness that decimated the heroic confidence of
Ignatius as he entered Manresa. In the clutches of this helplessness, all he could do was cry out to God. But in those depths he
was purified of the selfishness that was eating its way into the love
response he felt. In one of the most important discoveries of his
life, he learned to entrust himself completely to a Savior who alone
could rescue him. Cusson sums up Ignatius's experience in the
first four months of Manresa as "a realization that he was totally
incapable of achieving, by his own efforts alone, the salvation and
sanctification which he ambitioned. Through this painful purification which he details in his *Autobiography*, he discovers the meaning of spiritual evangelical poverty."[2]

In the third stage, teetering on the brink of the horror of evil and sin, calling out for help, you fall into the merciful love of God in Jesus. The horror of sin brings not your annihilation but an utterly undeserved gift of forgiveness. Just so, Ignatius learned that in the depths of his helplessness, he was not abandoned and condemned, but forgiven. From the trust born in the face of such helplessness, a whole life of pilgrim reliance and intimacy grew for him. As you penetrate the difficulty at the end of the Foundation, you will trace the journey of Ignatius, trusting in a gift that becomes a whole life.

Second Overview: A Divine Intervention

In an article titled "The First Week of the Spiritual Exercises," Winoc De Broucker states, "The First Week is an intervention of God in our lives, a divine halt which judges and interrupts the course of our daily lives."[3] Some reflection on the experience of making an intervention in the life of someone enmeshed in the web of substance abuse can give you a helpful view of what you are now beginning.

A formal intervention is a serious and difficult step taken only when it is clear that a friend is caught, probably unconsciously, in a web of deceit and is acting in a way that is destructive of self. The trap of the addiction is usually sealed with sincere denial on the part of this person. As a result, a simple mentioning in passing of the issue will have no effect. A formal case for intervention must be prepared.

The people making the intervention must show clearly their genuine, personal love and care for their friend; otherwise, the hard truth of the intervention will not find a hearing. The case for intervention cannot involve a vague, general claim but must be concrete, with dates, times, and numbers. The interveners must express a desire for life and thus an end to the destructive activity. Finally, they must express that, because of their love and concern for their friend, they are the people being most hurt by this addictive behavior and denial.

This brief description of a formal intervention gives you a good picture of God's work with you in the First Week. The dramatic conclusion of the prophet Nathan's confrontational parable to David catches the breakthrough of an intervention: "Then Nathan said to David, 'You are the man. . . .' David said to Nathan, 'I have sinned against Yahweh.' Then Nathan said to David, 'Yahweh, for his part, forgives your sin; you are not to die'" (2 Sm 12:7–14). In 1 John 1:10 also, an intervention seems called for: "For if we take up the attitude 'we have not sinned,' we flatly deny God's diagnosis of our condition and cut ourselves off from what he has to say to us."[4]

Third Overview: A Rude Awakening before the Cross

At the end of the Foundation, the mystery of Christ is experienced as glory, the glory of God's love, resounding from the first moment of creation into the future fullness of time. Now, suddenly, at the end of the first meditation in this part of the Exercises, you are confronted with the horrendous spectacle of this glorious Christ nailed to a tree, ignominiously humiliated in crucifixion. The shock of this discovery is indescribable. To come upon Jesus Christ as an old man in his eighties peacefully laid out in a coffin would be sad enough. But the rude awakening before a young, crucified Christ screams the questions, "How? Why?"

In stark simplicity the prayer of this First Week will answer the questions. You, and all of us, are responsible for his being crucified; and yet this dismal scene epitomizes the greatest act of love anyone will ever do for us. You must pray long enough through this part until both of these answers deeply engrave themselves on your heart.

Peace in a Murky, Darksome Part of Yourself

The three overviews above reveal that this part of the retreat has a fearful, difficult quality and yet promises a loving peace. A murky, troubling area lies in all our hearts. It frightens and shames us, but it will not go away. We are not proud of ourselves; our failures discourage and depress us, so we distract ourselves and stay away from that charged area. We are certainly not ready in public to admit its existence, let alone talk about it. (Though at times this area is wisely taken to a therapist, I am not referring here to anything psychologically abnormal.)

A longing to be healed, to be at peace, is also surfacing. Sometimes this longing verges on the impossible hope that this whole area will just go away. But for the most part, we go on drowning out the sound of these unnerving feelings in our distracted, busy lives. We can continue to do many good things and lead a responsible life of service, but inside we know that something is missing. In the First Week of the Exercises we are invited to wade into this murky area on the promise of finding revealed in its shadowy depth the peace of Jesus Christ.

Reflecting on Your Own Experience

Shame, sorrow, and apology figure prominently in this experience with God. To reflect on your previous experience of these dynamics in interpersonal relationships can be a helpful introduction. Can you remember when you were ashamed of and sorry for something you said or did? You may have been tempted to repress and forget these feelings because they seem draining and not productive for your future. However, sometimes you lingered in them and felt a need to apologize to the one harmed by your misdeed.

Apologizing is risky because you must admit to yourself and to another that you were wrong. Some people cannot do this. They never apologize to anybody for anything. It damages their image. The secular ideal of a confident, self-sufficient, productive person cannot risk wasting psychic energy in the dynamics of shame, sorrow, and apology. But if you have ever faced the call echoing in your shame and sorrow to initiate an apology, then you have some sense of the dynamics at work with God in this part of the Exercises.

Apologizing out of healthy shame and sorrow always matures and deepens the intimacy of love between friends. To overlook the misdeed in the thought that time will heal it never matures human love.

The Grace Desired

Ignatius does not view sin in any simple, superficial fashion. The grace desired is not simply an honest, thorough listing of your sins compiled as quickly as possible in readiness for confession. Ignatius looks at sin not as a moralistic examination of conscience, nor simply with a psychological concern about limitations to freedom, nor just in a purely mathematical concern for numbers, nor, finally, only in a sociological and anthropological concern for the effect within the human family.

In the words of Michael Ivens, S.J., Ignatius pushes through to a "rigorously and explicitly theocentric view of sin. . . . The *Exercises* are concerned not so much with sins as with the sin within the sins, not with the immediately obvious reality but with the hidden reality of the *mysterium iniquitatis,* the mystery of evil."[5] Before facing the details of your sins, you are begging for insight into the meaning of sin itself. Sin from God's perspective more closely approaches the truth than does sin from our perspective. The self-protective spirit in us all tends to rationalize and play down the significance of sin. Only God can reveal this truthful view, if we genuinely desire it.

The context for this revelation of sin's meaning is framed in the Foundation and your experience of God's creative, intimate love. From this perspective sin has an objectivity beyond your own awareness. "Sin is a frightful ingratitude on the part of the creature toward his or her all-loving Creator," as Cusson presents it.[6] To let this objective reality pierce through the net of rationalization that we use to overlook or justify our sin takes time. It also presumes that your relationship with your loving Creator is still alive in your heart, because, finally, it is the presence of God's gracious love that reveals your sin. So often in the past, unhealthy, shameful influences have shaken the finger of guilt in your face regarding sin. Here the experience is quite different. Within your growing awareness of sin, something profoundly personal and hopeful is at work. The fire of God's love is inviting you insistently into the deep glow of peace and the radiant energy of salvation in Christ Jesus. Your own memory and willpower cannot produce this revelation. Without a lively sense of God's love, this revelation of sin is not possible. In that situation the problem lies not with God but with your complacent sense of the Creator's immediate, intimate love.

In his first exercise in this week, Ignatius leads you back through the long history of creaturely ingratitude from the very beginning up to your own present moment. In rehearsing this long history, at least four insights come: you recognize your own personal history; you get insight into the social dynamics of sin in our contemporary age; you get a sense of how widespread the mystery of sin is; and, most important, you gradually sense the effect of all of this on your gracious, loving Creator. You begin to share God's own confusion and sorrow in the face of so much ingratitude. This is no pleasure trip but can bring tears to your heart and your eyes.

From this you learn to distinguish between a salvific and an unsalvific sense of sin. In the salvific sense of sin, a saving God is leading you deeper into Christ Jesus. In an unsalvific sense, two divergent options can occur. First, a mild or flagrant arrogance comes to the same conclusion: no sin. Second, a lack of healthy self-love or, even worse, a self-loathing exaggerates both your guilt and the number of sins. The grace begged for here, as Ignatius describes it, is a development from "shame and confusion" to "a growing and intense sorrow and tears for my sins."[7] As mentioned earlier, in some way this grace is a sharing in the Creator's own confusion and sorrow before the long history of creaturely ingratitude. As the frightfulness of this ingratitude dawns on you, your soul blushes in a healthy sense of guilt and shame, something very different from self-hatred. None of this feels nice; a deep pain and discomfort pervade the grace given here. The graced confusion prayed for here includes a wonder and awe that after such frightful ingratitude the Creator, rather than angrily destroying you, continues to love in care and hope. Such a response to sin stretches your soul.

Your sin's effect before your loving Creator is not some vague, cosmic confusion and sorrow. At the closing colloquy of the first exercise, Ignatius brings you quickly before Jesus on the cross. To stand in your responsibility before Jesus dying on the cross brings a sorrow that simmers in your heart and drops you to your knees. The suffering and death of God's Son for your sin and his words of forgiveness are a clear revelation both of the frightful reality of sin and of a powerfully transforming forgiveness.

At the core of God's forgiveness in Jesus is a painful, humiliating purification. Like a fire cauterizing the egotistical wound of sin, the grace of forgiveness heals with hope for the future. Without the painful humiliation and purification, the forgiving grace cannot pierce deeply into your heart and remains more a surface solution without much hope for the future. You can imagine how quickly and subtly your heart will be tempted to blunt and slight this painful balm of forgiveness.

The Goal of the First Week

The First Week, finally, is all about God's loving forgiveness for ungrateful sinners. This forgiveness is very costly on God's part, as the cross makes clear. It is also undeserved on our part. For this reason the grace of shame, confusion, and sorrow does not linger in your heart but is reconfigured in a new identity: gratitude. The colloquies in two of the five exercises of this week explicitly mention gratitude. The precious gift of forgiveness in the pit of your helplessness in sin practically explodes in gratitude, laying a foundation for a whole style of living. God's forgiveness goes far beyond anything we could do for ourselves and far beyond any legitimate claim we can make on God. Yet the gift so gratuitously given is what our hearts most long for: salvation, life, service, and glorious peace beyond death.

At the end of the third exercise Ignatius presents a triple colloquy, a friendly conversation that involves a challenging grace especially difficult in our contemporary age.[8] He advises you to pray for an *abhorrence* both for your sins and for the vain and worldly spirit that infects human reality. This concept can seem strange or old-fashioned; we may even wonder if it is possible. Our reflective sensitivity helps us to learn valuable lessons from our sinning—

patience, trust, and reliance on God. Thus sin can seem good, jus-
tified because of its valuable lessons.

But God has a passionate hatred for sin. The death of God's
Son on the cross reveals that. God also always has a passionate forgiving love for all sinners. The cross makes that clear too. In the
grace offered here, you are invited to share God's love for you, a
love that is so great as to abhor the slightest ungrateful response.
To pray for this grace stretches the desire of your soul and makes
possible an amendment of self that has more hope of holding. The
wind of the Holy Spirit is stretching the sails of your soul to a tautness and a sturdiness capable of a flexibility focused for a new, lasting direction.

The fifth exercise of this part is an application of your senses to
the horror of hell. Many times in the past this type of prayer has
been misused, stirring a fright that was neither salvific nor healthy.
In his commentary, Michael Ivens, S.J., has words of insight to
guide us: "The meditation on hell is not for Ignatius the starting-
point of conversion, but a confirmation. It comes after the exercitant has had the experience of God's merciful love."[9]

If this meditation began the whole First Week, it would lay a
wobbly foundation for conversion. But by the end of the week the
conversion has been worked by grace in the awareness of your
ingratitude and God's astonishing response of forgiveness. Now
the possibility of a hell confirms the conversion both in the graced
fear of any separation from God and in thankfulness for divine
patience and forgiveness.

A dramatic contemporary image can help you to perceive the
tone of this week as it comes to a conclusion. Imagine the fear of
someone trapped in a burning building: such a crumbling before
death's advance is terrible even to ponder. But what if the person
regains consciousness outside the building and learns that someone

provided a rescue? You can imagine that person's surprise, disorientation, amazement, and, finally, deep-hearted dedication to the rescuer. The debt of gratitude would stretch as far as life itself.

The First Week brings you on your knees before Jesus on the cross. He is God's forgiveness. He is your life. He has saved you from the death of sin. This realization stretches your soul wide. At the nadir of your helplessness, Jesus reached out and rescued you. Your gratitude and commitment to Jesus lay the foundation for your conversion into a new identity. You are linked to him for life. The problem and difficulty that conflicted with your desire to be faithful at the end of the Foundation have been resolved in Jesus on the cross. Now it dawns on you that you can be faithful, never on your own, but always and only in Christ.

The End of the First Week

This part of the Exercises does not conclude but flows right into the Second Week. Aware of being a forgiven crucifier, you stand now bathed in gratitude and joy before Jesus on the cross. As I have described this experience before, "The humiliation of forgiveness chastens the soul's sight to recognize God, beautiful in Jesus, present and at work in all."[10] This recognition warms the heart to a respectful and gentle reverence toward God, self, others, and all of reality.

With a whole new lease on life, your heart desires to know your Redeemer much more intimately. In fact, your one great desire is to find your own unique way of serving with him in the development of greater glory in our universe. To be faithful to that revealed vocation and role of service is your very life.

You are before the cross in a wide-open abandonment of self in response to so much love. As long as your eyes are off yourself and on him, you know the excitement of a freedom for whatever Jesus desires for you, beyond any bargaining. This is a wide-open consolation unfurling the sails of your truest self before God. This stance of bracing freedom, this readiness for whatever Jesus may desire for you, is an important foundation on which to stand and on which to base your life. This is the touchstone of freedom that makes possible all future discernment. Without this foundation of freedom, discernment is always questionable. When your eyes fall from Jesus and settle more on yourself, you can be fixated, without even realizing it, on your concern instead of his.

You have been humbled in a way that raises you up in a new identity of soul and desire. As one defense after another has fallen, you know now that you are not as good as you have worked hard for years to make yourself seem, but you are much more loved than you could ever have imagined. You are left in and with Jesus as the love of your life. But you desire to know him much better, especially in your own unique way. The experience will—indeed must—go on.

The Role of Confession

Ignatius's own practice invited a general confession as the best way to sacramentalize the conversion of the First Week of the Exercises. His own experience of conversion in the castle at Loyola led him to the Benedictine monastery on Montserrat and three days of preparation for a general confession, which turned him away from his sinful past and toward God leading him to Manresa.

This use of a general confession served an important pastoral purpose for the early Jesuits in the sixteenth century. In a church responding to the Reformation, confession often acquired a legalistic quality that stirred an unhealthy anxiety and guilt. In this atmosphere the early Jesuits exercised an important ministry of consolation by leading people through a miniversion of the First Week, culminating in the pastoral experience of a general confession that brought the consolation of God's merciful love. John O'Malley, S.J., states it this way: "Conversion of heart was, of course, not exactly a new idea in Christianity. What the general confession did, however, was to provide a mode in which it could be articulated, ritualized, and blessed."[11]

With sails unfurled and billowing loudly in the exciting wind, your soul stretches for more before a Redeemer whose rescue on a cross has marked you for life. This readies you for the Kingdom exercise described in the next chapter.

5

Readied for Wise Loving

Afterthe First Week, the exercise about the call of Christ the King serves as a bridge between what you have already experienced and what lies ahead. It renews and tests the durability of your new graced self, and it prepares you for future challenge. The Foundation and First Week have changed a number of things: how you view reality, how you relate to God, how you respond to Jesus on the cross. However much you feel incomplete and in need of further development, your soul has been stretched to a new self.

Gilles Cusson speaks of a movement of soul that is of seismic proportions. In the movement from the snare of infinite ingratitude in sin to an infinite gratitude in Jesus on the cross, God's grace has worked a tremor of soul and reorganized the "plates" deep in your identity, thereby healing a fault line. It is an extraordinary journey, one that could only be propelled by God. From our vantage point, such a saving reconfiguration happened in a most shocking and unlikely way—through the death of God in the person of Christ.[1]

The first exercise of the First Week concluded with a colloquy on the energizing encounter with Jesus on the cross, in which Ignatius posed three questions for consideration: What have I done for Christ? What am I doing for Christ? What must I do for

Christ?[2] They are the questions of someone who has come into a whole new orientation of life. They are part of getting your bearings and gradually settling into this new relationship. The first two questions are capable of definite answers. The third, however, is an exclamation of soul and is not meant to be answered now; to feel the fire of the question is enough. It is the wonder and exclamation of a lover, more aware of the beloved than ever before.

Forgiveness for a trapped sinner is the birthplace of zeal for ministry and the desire to serve. When the forgiven sinner rests in self-contented delight, the natural dynamic of the experience has misfired and been waylaid. "What must I do?" catches the thrust of forgiveness. This exercise of the call of Christ the King will test your new identity.

Signs of Readiness to Enter the Second Week

Ignatius did not automatically move everyone on to the Second Week. He was always looking for a special giftedness of soul and eagerness of heart—the *magis* desire that ends the Foundation—as signs that a person was called to continue.

The heart's graced desire for more is a first sign of readiness to continue. As this desire begins to take hold in your heart, you are not content with simply being forgiven. Encountering Jesus on the cross stretches this basic desire: to know him more and to discover the unique relationship you are to have with him. No ordinary discipleship will do. A desire to be heroic stirs in your heart. To stop the journey now would frustrate your desire for an intimacy and generosity unique to yourself. This part of the Exercises introduces the experience of falling in love with Jesus. It is the grace running through the rest of the experience.

A capacity for intimacy opens the door for a full-hearted reception of this grace and is, therefore, a second sign of readiness to proceed. A person deprived of any experience of human intimacy will be robbed of an important dimension of the rest of the retreat. If intimacy is something only thought about, then a love relationship can tend to settle in the head more than in the heart. In his book *Being Sexual—and Celibate,* Keith Clark describes intimacy as involving three elements: self-awareness, self-disclosure, and careful mutual listening.[3]

Without the solid foundation of a clear sense of identity, intimacy is always elusive. A self that you confidently realize and possess makes mature relationships possible. Your experience in the Foundation and First Week revealed a new self. Then comes the choice of whether you will cling to that self for its own sake or share the gift with others—risking rejection or even ridicule. To avoid the risk is to forfeit the opportunity for intimacy. A humble confidence about self equips you to face this risk.

Intimacy also involves being together in self-disclosure and respectful listening. As the Exercises proceed, these activities will produce an intimate companionship between you and Jesus. Although intimacy in love defies your firm control, it does have a role for the mind. But more important, it always involves your full person in the presence of a special encounter. A retreatant whose life has already known intimacy in relationship obviously brings to this part of the Exercises an important background of experience.

Besides the two signs of a desire to know Jesus in your unique vocation and capacity for intimacy, a third sign of readiness here is some personal lived experience of the need for salvation and liberation in the social dimension of our world. An utter insensitivity to the oppression and injustice in our world can limit your experience of the

Exercises to the narrow world of self. To have seen and felt the social injustice in our world, on the other hand, intensifies your awareness of the world's need for salvation. As the Exercises continue, Ignatius provides meditations that highlight this social perspective.

From one perspective, the call of the King provides some of this social orientation. The words *all* and *whole* punctuate the text with a frequency that stretches the focus widely beyond the individual self. The temporal king and Christ the King issue a call for a universal salvation that requires the shared sacrifice of many followers. In the heat of the crying need for justice and freedom, a professionally conceived and executed plan of social transformation provides much-needed help but is not, in itself, the saving grace of Christ. The relationship of social analysis and action to the faith perspective of salvation in Christ is something we will return to later in the book.

Ignatius: Loyola to Manresa

This exercise of the call of the King allows you to share Ignatius's experience as his conversion grew from Loyola to Manresa. As mentioned earlier, Ludolph of Saxony, rather than providing leisure reading during convalescence, brought Ignatius into a thorough encounter with the mystery of Christ (see chapter 1). Though the magnet was not turned full face on him yet, the pieces of his life were rearranged as a new foundation was being laid.

As he moved geographically, his spiritual journey was manifested in certain dramatic externals. He exchanged his own clothes of nobility for a poor man's simple sacklike garment and pilgrim's staff. He got rid of his donkey and let his hair and nails grow untended. These externals had value in opposing and reversing previous proud concerns of his heart, but too much of Ignatius still controlled and colored these gestures.

Manresa was the furnace of purification that painfully burned away the selfish dross as Ignatius was drawn even more deeply into the fire of the Divine Majesty.[4] The competitive aspect of his loving was left in charred ruins. He exits Manresa with the pieces of his life wholly rearranged through his full exposure to the Cardoner River magnet. Now he is not fiercely engaged in competition with anyone. The Divine Majesty who rescued him from the throes of helplessness has completely taken over his heart. Life will be intimate companionship with the beloved in loving—full-throttled loving—but not as decided on his own.

The heroism now is more quiet, patient, wise, discerning. He is becoming more and more a *caballero de Dios* ("knight of God"). He would still love heroically but only in the special way that the Divine Majesty revealed *de arriba* ("from above") as appropriately unique for him. *De arriba* is a key phrase in Ignatius's theology.[5] It speaks of his experience of God's transcendent love as beyond all other, but a love that has embraced him into a companionship and stretched his freedom to find God literally in all things. The raging fire of Loyola has been trimmed and focused much more precisely. The flame will burn, but now more quietly and steadily, awaiting the Divine Majesty's gentle breeze *de arriba,* revealing the discerned nuance of God's greater glory for Ignatius's uniquely greater service. Ignatius comes out of Manresa humbled, quieted. But the fire has not gone out. Whereas it might have quickly burned itself out leaving Loyola, now after Manresa the flame burns quietly, steadily, focused on the Divine Majesty. Ignatius's whole energy is gathered, awaiting the lead of the Divine Majesty so he can follow in a love that will not competitively outburn others but will serve discerningly. Discreet, discerning love has refined, nuanced, captured his heart.

An example from Ignatius's life helps to make the point here.[6] In his prayer of earlier years, he was weeping so profusely that his eyesight was endangered. As soon as a doctor pointed this out, Ignatius heard a call to forgo the tears of his prayer for the sake of his unique service of God's greater glory. His wisely discerning love of God at Manresa had set his heart so thoroughly on God and given him a freedom of indifference so all-extensive as to enable him to separate the pure reality of God from any mystical experiences of the divinity. In such heroic freedom, therefore, he could hear in the doctor's caution a call of the Divine Majesty. In the early stage of profuse heroic love at Loyola, this would have seemed a stupid, ungenerous gesture of useless sacrifice.

The Kingdom Exercise

The Kingdom exercise prepares you for the coming Second, Third, and Fourth Weeks. In your experience of the Foundation and the First Week, the pieces of your own life were rearranged in line with a radical conversion. You know that your life is different and that, from now on, your heart must love. The question that fills your heart is, What must I do for Christ? This power of graced generosity cannot be dismissed, but the thrust of self, even in the question just reiterated, will be purified and refined. Thus, the goal is not how you must love but what the Divine Majesty reveals as your discerned unique way of loving.

The grace of this Kingdom exercise is aimed at this subtler, more nuanced loving. You are asked to pray for the grace to "not be deaf to his call, but ready and diligent to accomplish his most holy will."[7] It is the grace of careful listening to our Lord, a grace that carries you through the remainder of the retreat and sets up the possibility of increasing intimacy with Jesus. Therefore, through the transitional orientation of this exercise, the magnetic call of Christ grows, sharpens, and, finally, dominates the rest of the retreat.

The Mission to Love

The Third Point. I will consider what good subjects ought to respond to a king so generous and kind; and how, consequently, if someone did not answer his call, he would be scorned and upbraided by everyone and accounted as an unworthy knight.

The Second Part of This Exercise

**consists in applying
the above parable of a temporal king
to Christ our Lord
according to the three points just mentioned.**

The First Point. If we give consideration to such a call from the temporal king to his subjects, how much more worthy of our consideration it is to gaze upon Christ our Lord, the eternal King, and all the world assembled before him. He calls to them all, and to each person in particular he says: "My will is to conquer the whole world and all my enemies, and thus to enter into the glory of my Father. Therefore, whoever wishes to come with me must labor with me, so that through following me in the pain he or she may follow me also in the glory."

The Second Point. This will be to reflect that all those who have judgment and reason will offer themselves wholeheartedly for this labor.

The Third Point. Those who desire to show greater devotion and to distinguish themselves in total service to their eternal King and universal Lord, will not only offer their persons for the labor, but go further still. They will work against their human sensitivities and against their carnal and worldly love, and they will make offerings of greater worth and moment, and say:

"Eternal Lord of all things, I make my offering, with your favor and help. I make it in the presence of your infinite Goodness, and of your glorious Mother, and of all the holy men and women in your heavenly court. I wish and desire, and it is my deliberate decision, provided only that it is for your greater service and praise, to imitate you in bearing all injuries and affronts, and any poverty, actual as well as spiritual, if your Most Holy Majesty desires to choose and receive me into such a life and state."[8]

The call of the King sounds the great mission to love. All human hearts are sensitive to this call. The parable of the earthly king is Ignatius's way, from his experience of the chivalric ideal of his times, of pointing to the powerful, magnetic effect that love has on us all. The power of jealousy rushing to violence and murder on the part of jilted lovers bears sad but frequent testimony to the captivating hold that love has on our hearts.

In the First Week the loving of our own heart was reoriented and intensified in the face of the awesomely generous fierce love of Jesus on the cross. In the second part of this exercise, Christ the King radiates his mission—to share the fulfilling love and glory of his Beloved with everyone. His desire is a call for helpers who will labor with him in this enterprise. This call and its attractiveness will increase and be uniquely specified for you as the retreat continues. Here, in the words Ignatius puts on the lips of Christ, you hear a renewal of the objective revelation of the mystery of Christ. The string of your foundational experience of God's love in Christ is plucked once again, resonating loud and clear.

The next two points in the text describe a growing response of generous love and echo with elements of Ignatius's conversion stretching from Loyola to Manresa. The objective revelation of the mystery of Christ elicits a wide spectrum of subjective responses from simple refusal to a generous, mature following. In the second point, the response is one enlightened in faith and moved "wholeheartedly" by the encounter with Jesus Christ. This response, positive and wholeheartedly generous, rings with Ignatius's own heroic response as he strode out of Loyola. The third point develops this response to something more sensitive and mature. Beyond a quick, emotional generosity comes the realization of the inner struggle involved in full discipleship. The original superficial generosity is deepening and maturing in wisdom, in a process similar to Ignatius's development at Manresa.

The sample offering of self that Ignatius proposes is something new in the Exercises at this point. It is not an assignment that must be done. No, you must make the offering to Christ the King that is in your own heart. You may not be feeling all that is in Ignatius's sample; do not offer what, at this point, has not yet been given to you. Your offering should be articulated generously in the intimacy of colloquy with Christ the King and recorded in your own journal.

But this offering, carefully delineated by Ignatius, should be closely read, even parsed word by word, to feel the thrust for the future of your experience.[9] The offering is addressed to the "Eternal Lord of all things," a title and vision for Jesus beyond that of Creator and Savior. It is a new title at this point in the *Exercises* but points to the development of the coming three parts.

An element of the willfulness representative of Ignatius's generosity at Loyola is present early in the offering: "I wish and desire, and it is my deliberate decision." But this willfulness, purified at Manresa, is now qualified and nuanced: "provided only that it is for your greater service and praise" and "if your Most Holy Majesty desires to choose and receive me into such a life and state." Another phrase points you into the Second Week, which you are about to begin: "to imitate you in bearing all injuries and affronts, and any poverty, actual as well as spiritual."

This example of an offering of self to Christ the King is not meant to be a throwaway or the prescribed close of this exercise. Rather, it serves as a preface bridging your previous experience of the Foundation and First Week with your coming experience of the Second Week. A preface is usually written after a book has been completed; so it is here with Ignatius. Only after his own purifying and maturing experience at Manresa could he articulate this preface of the Kingdom, with its concluding illuminative and challenging offering of self.

As you move into the Second Week, your heart stirs with great generosity before Jesus on the cross, resonates with the call of Christ the King, and listens carefully for a further development of your generosity. Your encounter of falling in love with Jesus will immerse you ever more deeply into the Divine Majesty and bring a balanced integration of generosity and discernment as you share God's vision for the glory of the whole universe.

You have been rescued from a burning building. Now, rather than just walking away in eternal gratitude, you are being invited to reenter the building to help in the rescue of all the others still trapped.

6

A School of Discipleship

The Second Week is a school of discipleship. In discipleship you enter into a relationship that leads you deeply into the sentiments, thoughts, and values of another person. This school requires patience, fueled by a great desire to know the other person. Though discipleship provides many values in itself, it is usually preparation for something else. In the Exercises the discipleship of the Second, Third, and Fourth Weeks readies you for apostleship. An apostle is someone sent out in the name of the one sending. The danger for apostles is that they get distracted and preach as though sent in their own name. When this occurs, it always reveals a failure in discipleship. It takes time for love to pull you out of your own selfish ground and plant you in the attractive garden of another person. But, finally, the sign of genuine love is that you become whom you love.

In this Second Week you will learn to love and serve discerningly with the more probing sensitivity and subtlety of the Second Week discernment rules.[1] The grace of the Kingdom continues to invite you to place yourself humbly, reverently, generously, and attentively in God's school of discipleship, which focuses on Jesus as risen Lord of all history. The teaching here will not require blackboard and chalk or computer and software. It occurs through entering an interpersonal relationship. Ignatius described himself as taught by God "as a schoolmaster treats a little boy when he teaches him."[2] This unique, profound, personal learning stretches beyond book knowledge. The Second Week centers on contemplation of Jesus. Becoming whom we contemplate is a beautiful yet challenging way of learning another person as that person's values, mentality, and heart take flesh in ourselves.

The danger as you move into this Second Week is impatience. In a freedom before Jesus on the cross beyond any freedom you have ever known before, you can be eager to make your own decisions and rush on with your life. This short-circuiting of discipleship for the sake of apostleship risks the toppling of your life into the quicksand of your own concerns. The Second Week involves a waiting for the energy of "what you must do for Christ" to grow into a sensitivity for recognizing whatever the Divine Majesty reveals *de arriba*. Neither contemplation nor love can be rushed. They are hard work. But it is a work well worth the effort because it provides an intimacy that expands your heart. Your own unique role in the expansiveness of God's loving glory will be revealed by the Divine Majesty *de arriba* in your contemplative composure before the mystery of Christ.

Ignatian Contemplation

The style of Ignatian prayer is easily misunderstood, both within and outside the Jesuit tradition. A multiplicity of directives, techniques, and methods can distract you from the fundamental dynamic and orientation actually intended. Ignatian prayer is a progressive concentration and assimilation of a person's energies and powers in an encounter of love with God in Jesus. Primarily neither contemplative nor meditative, the heart of Ignatian prayer is this progressive assimilation. The types of prayer in the *Exercises* move you from consideration to meditation, to contemplation, to repetition, to application of senses. This development draws you gradually into the simplicity and intimacy of the encounter with Jesus. But serious consideration is not enough. The simple gazing and intimate presence of contemplation must be repeated with ever more personal focus, and thus spill over into the sensual application of psychosexual energies. In this way your person is affected in your deepest, most intimate and practical dimensions. Only in this way can a personal transformation happen that has any hope of lasting.

This progressively personal assimilation also forges a special contemplative presence in daily life. Contemplation, while it can soar to great heights, must finally walk in "the joys and hopes, the griefs and the anxieties . . . of this age."[3] A saying attributed to the Carmelite William McNamara states, "Contemplation takes a long loving look at the real."[4] With the eyes of Jesus, contemplation, therefore, finds God's glory everywhere.

As I noted in an article on contemplation, "In the Ignatian method of prayer, as in all contemplation—and in any genuine love too—we become whom we contemplate."[5] In his book *Living Jesus,* Luke Timothy Johnson describes the process of learning another person.[6] This is quite different from learning *about* another person. It inspires a much more personal, intimate knowledge. To learn the person is to enter that person's heart. This process, according to Johnson, involves trust, respect, attentiveness, meditating in silence, patience, suffering, and creative fidelity. Obviously, growth in this knowing takes time.

In the Second Week, contemplation will help you to learn Jesus, to enter the tabernacle of his heart, to encounter him in an intimate and zealous faith. This is the grace Ignatius has you pray for here: "an interior knowledge of Our Lord, who became human for me, that I may love him more intensely and follow him more closely."[7] The inner dynamic of this grace integrates the three aspects of knowing, loving, and following into the unified and personal relationship of a disciple. To know someone in the way described here is to love and to follow that person almost irresistibly. This is a process both of self-transformation and of union with the beloved.

Jesus as Your Lord

In the Foundation, you experienced Jesus as your Creator; in the First Week, you experienced him as Savior. Here the grace is to know him as Lord. In Paul's letter to the Philippians (2:9–11) the triumph is described this way: "But God raised him high and gave him the name which is above all other names . . . that every tongue should acclaim Jesus Christ as Lord, to the glory of God the Father." The Resurrection crowns the whole earthly life of Jesus with the lordship of all history. The risen Jesus, no one else, is Lord of all reality. So if you are to know him as Lord, you must be with him all through the journey that constitutes him as Lord.

These contemplations of the life of Jesus are often misunderstood. Some people think they are invited to go back two thousand years and try to imagine a scene that is long since dead and gone. However, these Ignatian contemplations are salvific experiences of the risen Jesus, personally present right now in the Spirit to you and to us all.[8]

Indeed, the past is present in us now. All of us in our identity are constituted by all the experiences we have ever had. Most of us forget many of these experiences, so they are not available to us. But it is different with the risen Jesus. As Son of God, filled uniquely with the Holy Spirit, the risen Jesus remembers every jot and tittle of his experience. Nothing escapes his memory.

That means Jesus' experiences are present to us. For example, contemplating the baptism of Jesus at the Jordan is a matter of listening attentively as the risen Jesus shares that experience with you. Jesus' experience begins with the details of the Gospel account and continues as the description is filled out and personalized for you through the inspiration of the Holy Spirit. These Gospel scenes and events are salvific right now; rather than one-dimensional historical events, they are available as lively mysteries in your relationship with the risen Jesus.

You must learn to take these Gospel accounts very seriously, as encounters with the risen Jesus, as up-to-date as the moment when you enter the prayer. Ignatius recommends the use of imagination as a way into the mystery. Not everyone's imagination is pictorial, but imagination is the capacity we all have that helps us to relive an experience with a special personal vividness. In these contemplations the Holy Spirit is eager to engage you with the various mysteries of the risen Jesus by stirring your unique practice of imagination. The contemplation desired here is much more than a superficial replaying of a past historical event. Rather, the Holy Spirit effects an engagement of your whole person with the mystery in an encounter with the risen Jesus. Growing personal composition of yourself with the mystery, a deepening personal entry into the mystery, gathers over time into the interior, intimate knowledge for which you are praying. In this way the mystery is happening right now, and you, as more than an objective spectator, are participating firsthand.

For Ignatius this type of contemplating with the help of Gospel scenes worked purification in his fantasy life, which had been filled to overflowing with romantic courtly love imagery. It transformed his fantasy life with an imagery of a new love and a new beloved. Something similar happens for you during these contemplations. Love emerges and grows before becoming an object of reflection. Love grabs hold spontaneously and engages our psychic and imaginative energy.

This composure of heart obviously is not limited to the times of prayer. It is not turned on and off at will but becomes habitual. A new identity is being formed in the beauty of Jesus. This new identity will find Jesus as the love of your heart. Ignatian contemplation, therefore, finds the God of Jesus in absolutely everything, through immersion into, rather than withdrawal from, the details of daily life.

Two Different Contemplations

The Second Week provides two different styles of contemplation—a descending and an ascending style. In the Incarnation, Ignatius places you in the heart of the creatively loving Trinity as God contemplates within the long history of humankind strains of blatant rebellion, complacent blindness, and lazy ignorance. As you watch with God, you hear echoing in the heart of the Trinity, "Let us work the redemption of the human race." Neither impatient anger nor frustrated spitefulness, but only love, will redeem. In the face of all that evil, a decision rises to send the Son to live as one of us in the very midst of our sinful world.

John's Gospel (3:16–17) says, "Yes, God loved the world so much that he gave his only Son. . . . not to condemn the world, but so that through him the world might be saved." It is an astonishing response. You need to stay, be with the Trinity in its contemplation of the sinful scene, and wonder at God's decision and election. Such wonder and awe can strip away any overfamiliarity that may have shrouded your heart regarding the Incarnation.

That decision for the Son to be sent as a human being rushes into a young Jewish girl named Mary. She is invited to be part of this redemptive mission. In this astonishing experience of God, Mary's affirmative response leaves her pregnant. A whole new stage of God's saving love has begun. For Ignatius the Incarnation and Annunciation are intimately linked. The Incarnation is news and event, not abstract metaphysical speculation.[9]

Notice the movement here. From the heart of the Trinity of God, the attention descends to the details of our sinful world and Mary's response: from God into the details of the world—a descending style of contemplation.

The movement is different in the next contemplation, on the Nativity. Here Ignatius inserts you into the earthy details of a laborious journey and birth. The attention is on the human people, what they are saying and doing. Through patient, reverent treasuring of these details, grace brings you to special insight. This birth, similar in setting to any number of others, is special. You realize that nothing in our world will ever be the same. After the human birth of this Creator-Friend, as the Holy Spirit brings this awareness, you are lifted up into the heart of God. Through a careful immersion into the details of a very human scene, you are drawn in an ascent to the loving heart of the Trinity.

Ignatius's words in this prayer serve as a good description of this simple style of contemplation: "I will make myself a poor, little, and unworthy slave, gazing at them, contemplating them, and serving them in their needs, just as if I were there, with all possible respect and reverence. . . . in order that the Lord may be born in greatest poverty; and that after so many hardships of hunger, thirst, heat, cold, injuries, and insults, he may die on the cross! And all this for me!"[10]

As you allow yourself to be drawn into the simple details of the concrete life of Jesus, that simplicity explodes with a reality awesome beyond words: the very inner life of God. Karl Rahner states the startling fact this way: "If in this concrete life of Jesus the inner life of God is revealed to us in an unsurpassable way, then a personal entering into this life of Jesus of Nazareth is a participation in the inner life of God; then the gaze into the face of Jesus of Nazareth is changed into the face-to-face vision of God, even if both the encounter with Jesus and the consequent vision of God only make their presence fully known when the confinement of our poor body is split wide open by death."[11]

These contemplations have a deceptive simplicity to them. As you contemplate the mysteries of Jesus through the rest of the retreat, you will develop your own style of contemplation, blending the descending and ascending movements Ignatius models in the first two mysteries.

These contemplations slowly but surely become an engagement with the risen Jesus that focuses the *magis* for you—your specially unique vocation for God's glory. In the Incarnation exercise, you see revealed in the Trinity what you yourself eagerly seek. In its contemplation of the mystery of sin, the Trinity finds surfacing an election, a decision for the Son to be sent for the redemption of the whole universe. Prayer on the Incarnation, startling in its own right, reveals the process you await as the retreat goes on.

Trinitarian Contemplations

For the remainder of the *Exercises* Ignatius boldly invites you to contemplate the Trinity of God, unique to the Christian revelation of God. God is the Trinity as focused in Jesus, God's Son become human, a brother to us all. Thus Christian religious experience is always Trinitarian. From the Second Week on, the object of the contemplations is the Trinity of God.

These contemplations concentrate on Jesus. But Jesus in an up-close, one-dimensional view loses the Trinitarian richness revealed in the mystery of Christ. To strip him of the love affair always burning in his heart is to lose his essential significance and to reduce him to a man of one season—a kind, compassionate servant, a social crusader for justice, or whatever you like—but not God's Son for all seasons. In these contemplations you encounter Jesus as given to you by the One he called "my dearly beloved Father." Simply to come upon Jesus in a particular human interpersonal setting is not enough. In each contemplation, the Holy Spirit leads you into the heart of Jesus and into the fire of love that enlightened, encouraged, and missioned him every step of the way. This Trinitarian perspective keeps each contemplation related to the Incarnation. Ignatius recommends this in the adaptation of the sixth practical directive for the Second Week: "frequently to call to mind the life and mysteries of Christ our Lord, from his Incarnation up to the place or mystery I am presently contemplating."[12]

The context of Jesus' journey from the Incarnation gives these mysteries their full orientation and direction. Each mystery details in a particular human interpersonal setting the astonishing salvific decision resonating in the heart of the Trinity. On this contemplative journey you are led into the heart of Jesus to find a whole Trinity of love. This process not only transforms you but inserts you into a new family—the family of God. This new family membership is captured in another of Ignatius's special phrases: *familiaritas cum Deo* ("a familiarity with God"). This family membership is implied in those opening words in the Foundation about the communal relationship of us all: "Human beings are created" (see chapter 3).

The special Trinitarian depth of these contemplations usually starts quite simply. Learn to treasure the details in the Gospel narrative, and be available for the Spirit's filling out of the mystery with additional details not articulated in the original account. These moments hold you in adoration and reverence as a recognition breaks through: here is God giving all in love to save you. Such moments both excite and quiet your heart in a reverent simplicity. Obviously, these moments are not meant to be rushed; they invite repetition and the sensual enchantment of tasting, touching, seeing, hearing, smelling divine loving intimacy. They are surely not under our control but are gratuitously given in God's mysterious providence.

Repetition growing into the intimacy of the application of senses plays an important regular role in this Second Week.[13] In this way your personal, unique penetration into the mysteries of Jesus' life touches the fire of God's love. A "once-over lightly" contemplation merely skims the surface. Repetition moving to sensual intimacy invites you to rest personally and profoundly in any detail of the mystery that beckons your heart.

Opening the eyes of your heart in the First Week amazed you with a whole new way of seeing. Here, in this Second Week, that new way of sensitive seeing brings into focus details of a mystery so attractive and absorbing as to reveal a new self and family membership for you.

As this Second Week goes on, your contemplative encounter with Jesus continues. However, the new seeing of your heart will be refined and sharpened now in an even clearer focus, leading to the revelation of your unique special vocation. Some distinctive Ignatian meditations will serve this purpose. In the next chapter I turn to the first of these, the meditation on the Two Standards.

7

A Cosmic Confrontation

In the ideal experience of the Exercises, the Second Week runs for twelve days. No set length is given for the Foundation and First Week because in Ignatius's practice this was part of his preparation of a person, which could take as long as a few years. Though the rate of movement in this first part varies with every person, many retreat houses set aside a period of about ten days before the first day of repose. A repose day lessens the intensity of the daily prayer schedule and provides opportunity for rest, relaxation, and conversation.

Early in the Second Week, on the fourth day, Ignatius inserts the meditation on the Two Standards, followed immediately by the meditation on the Three Classes of Persons. The Two Standards are the topic in the first four of five daily hours of prayer. No other meditation in the Exercises thus far has had this central place, and this detail in itself is a signal: you are at a central point in the whole experience. Though the other uniquely Ignatian meditations are obviously born of his experience and imaginative background, they also have roots in the Scriptures and thus are part of the mystery of Christ. These exercises, together with the call of Christ the King, relate to the purifying refinement that Manresa worked on Ignatius's unbounded generosity. Thus they are oriented to your *magis* desire—your eager desire for the revelation of a specially unique role in God's expansive process of loving glorification.

The meditation on the Two Standards proposes for your serious pondering a conflict swirling around in the consciousness of each of us. Though this conflict is enacted daily in your heart, its influence is much more extensive. What you meet in the privacy of your own heart flashes publicly across the whole universe in cosmic proportions: it is a confrontation of good and evil.

In the privacy of your inner life, no clear direction is imprinted as natural and right. The swirling fluctuation of your stream of consciousness can confuse and frustrate because no clear thrust stands out. A direction and orientation in life must be chosen and then followed. Without such a choice your life is up for grabs day after day. In a state of immaturity you flounder in yourself and are disturbingly unpredictable for others.

A Christian identity is not natural; no one at birth is a Christian. A choice, a decision encompassing a conversion and rebirth, is always necessary. For this reason Jesus begins his public life with the invitation, "Repent, and believe the Good News" (Mk 1:15). A whole new mindset is required. As Robert Barron points out, "Jesus urges his listeners to change their way of knowing, their way of perceiving and grasping reality, their perspective, their mode of *seeing*. . . . Soul transformation is Jesus' first recommendation."[1] This new birth is always accompanied by a dying. It involves the death of a previous approach and the missed opportunity of any number of other views of life. The death of a past self is never easy or painless.

The Two Standards call you into reflections of this sort. Ignatius uses the military image of an external standard, or banner, that gives direction on a battlefield. It is a good symbol, but it must be personalized in a particular mentality and attitude of heart. In paragraph 135 of the *Exercises,* Ignatius calls each standard an "intention." In the churning diversity of your consciousness, the choice is not among neutral options; rather, it is a choice between good and evil, between a Christlike and a satanic mentality. The stakes are as high as life and death.

We all have a "mentality of heart," even if we are not aware of it. A mentality, or way of viewing reality, is foundational to all human existence. Mentalities are very real; they exercise great influence on our hearts and actions, but they are also quite subtle—deceptively so. In this meditation, relying on the revelation of Scripture, Ignatius proposes that all mentalities are reduced to the central confrontation between good and evil, light and darkness, the Christlike and the satanic. Your interior life, however confusing it may seem at times, is charged with these opposing currents.

However, the conflict stretches far beyond your own inner life. The conflict you know in yourself is a focus, unique to you, of a conflict on a much grander scale. This conflict rages throughout the universe of planets and galaxies, races and genders, societies and nations, in the international and transnational organization of human affairs. As socially interactive beings, we live in the influence of our own inner world and in the socialization of that world of organized, international social patterns. Living within this interplay is our daily fare. It is also the field of battle for the two perspectives presented in this meditation. These two locations of battle must always be in view as you pray your way through the meditation on the Two Standards.

The Grace Desired

In the midst of a highly charged and treacherous battle, a standard provides the light of direction. Light and courage are precisely what are needed and are therefore the grace for which Ignatius has you pray. We must make a fundamental choice between the two standards. But the grace begged for is not to choose Jesus over Satan. That has happened already, or you would not be at this point in the Exercises. The grace here is an awareness of what your choice of Christ *actually involves for you.* You cannot avoid the cosmic conflict flashing daily through the universe. Your choice, rather, is whether you will be faithful and deal with the conflict.

Once again you need enlightenment and courage. Discernment of spirits is the grace Ignatius has you pray for as you ponder these two conflicting mentalities. To recognize in your heart and on the stage of civil society the deceitful, ensnaring ways of the one Ignatius calls "the enemy of human nature"[2] is an invaluable grace and piece of armor for the battle. Sometimes these evil ways involve gross and open temptations; other times a subtle temptation poses evil as good. To look through these subterfuges is not enough. You can look and not really see, and therefore do nothing about it. Spiritual enlightenment helps you to see what is really happening.

But enlightenment can remain theoretical and inactive. It is graced courage that provides the fire for spiritual enlightenment to take effect. At the same time, this courage alone, however generous it may seem, can be blind and misguided without the enlightenment really to see. Enlightenment and courage, as the grace desired here, mesh into a style of living: a mentality that sees and courage that acts on what is really seen. Some of the evil, dark, desolate ways have been catalogued in the Christian tradition as capital impulses to sin—those selfish, darksome signs in Galatians 5:19-21, which not only thrive in your consciousness but also are dramatized in our world and reported as news in papers and on television.

We also need insight into the way Christ is leading us. This way is difficult at times but always awash with genuine consolation. Because Christ's way is opposed to the satanic way of darkness, it might seem easy to detect. But it is not always easy. The mentality of Christ is usually countercultural and counter to many of the natural attractions in your heart. For this reason, you need great courage to choose the difficult option enlightened as Christ's loving truth.

An Apostolic Grace

As you pray your way through this meditation, some of the material dealt with in the First Week will return. But something is different. Here the issue is not sin, as in the First Week, but deception, where evil poses as an enticing good. Your experience of Jesus' forgiveness in the First Week tamed the sinful material but did not render it innocuous. The grace of this meditation over four hours of prayer reveals the deception lurking in the sinful ways of your heart and in the equally sinful ways of our world.

This meditation, with its power to show you how to see and respond courageously, is invaluable preparation for busy apostolic service. In the minefield of daily life your discernment will clear a way. An introspective absorption in self-perfectionism will always derail this meditation. The meditation on the Two Standards, with its unique enlightenment and courage, must be kept in close relationship with the Kingdom exercise.

Jerome Nadal, one of Ignatius's early companions, tells us that an extraordinary enlightenment of Ignatius at the Cardoner River while at Manresa is encapsulated in the two exercises of the Kingdom and the Two Standards. What Ignatius saw at the Cardoner was not about his own self-perfection but about the adventure

of furthering Christ's kingdom of love through a careful practice
of discernment.

This enlightenment about the two mentalities equips us to see
through the patterns and movements of our world. Professional
social analysis of policies in our world is valuable, yet this analysis
must always occur in the context of a faith vision. On the other
hand, a Christian faith vision can be naive and shortsighted if not
enlightened by professional social analysis. This grace keeps us
from becoming naive apostles.

This day's meditation on the Two Standards happens in the
midst of your growing contemplative love affair with the risen
Jesus. Because of this, the Two Standards cannot leave you
unmoved but stir you in a variety of ways. Your love for Jesus
matures in the refined balance of discerning love. The mentality of
Jesus is not some schema of accurate analysis but is the way of your
beloved. He issues an invitation for you to be with him in service.
Your experience of Jesus on the cross at the end of the First Week
is growing in detail and delineation. Even though this day on the
Two Standards can at first seem to interfere with the simple contemplative style of prayer, it provides an important background for
the remaining contemplations of the Second Week.

The Mentality of Satan

The mentality of Satan is completely self-focused and turned away
from God. This sounds as though it should be easily detected, but
it is usually well concealed. What you beg for in this meditation is
the grace to recognize it sooner. The universal pervasiveness of
Satan's mentality is symbolized in the frequent use of the words *all*
and *whole* as in the exercise on the Kingdom. Though "the leader

of all the enemy" is "horrible and terrifying,"[3] the dynamics of the approach are subtle and simulating.

The vulnerable point is a desire endemic to the human condition—the desire for riches. These riches are not necessarily financial. They can refer to your ambition for autonomy, to be somebody on your own, to take over and run your life your way. This mentality is a conviction that you are the meaning of your own life. This quietly motivating mentality can coexist with regular religious practice and belief in God. The enemy's assault is not gross and obvious at first; but an aroma of ambition thrills your soul, and your own hand is tightening its grip on the control of the sails of your life.

You know how strong is your need to be liked and well regarded. As you begin to steer the ship of your own life, your sails long for the bracing wind of other people's honor and respect. In fact, a drooping sail seems so discouraging that the needed breeze of public honor and affirmation sets off a dynamic of manipulation. You are working harder and harder to stretch the sails of your own life. You will do almost anything to have others applaud and think well of you. This manipulative way of dealing with other people, if not reflected on, can unconsciously begin to enslave you and squelch any genuine generosity out of most of your interpersonal relationships. When snared by this need for adulation, you begin to sense deep down a different breeze, a whisper of discontent. But the energetic adventure of keeping the sails of your life stretched and humming distracts you, and so you disregard the quiet whisper.

However inauspiciously this whole mentality may begin, it can so corrupt your heart that finally you yourself are the center and measure of everything. You are serving yourself as wholeheartedly as though you were a god. The desire to be like God, a gifted desire from the beginning, has collapsed into a very different desire: I want to *be* God. This condition of heart can continue to grow to what Ignatius calls "surging pride."[4] You have become the meaning of your own life. As mentioned before, this demonic and darkly selfish mentality is fueled by a demonic enemy, though you may be quite unaware of the whole development until late in the process. The subtlety of this development is the most insidious aspect of this attitude because, it must not be forgotten, this attitude, finally, leads to death.

In our contemporary world, we must consider an aspect of this process that Ignatius did not have to deal with—the relationship between spirituality and psychology. The psychology of human development can enrich the ideal of Christian spirituality, but psychology can also dethrone spirituality, with disastrous results. Similarly, spirituality can become hard and inhuman when completely segregated from psychology. Part of your challenge as you pray with the Two Standards is to relate these two mentalities to our contemporary appreciation of the art of human development.

Ignatius's final schematic presentation of the Two Standards can be reduced to two sets of three words: the mentality of Satan—*riches, honor, pride;* and the mentality of Christ—*poverty, contempt, humility.* However, you must penetrate the meanings of these words. In some situations today Ignatius's words can have a meaning exactly counter to what he intended. For people who live in degradation and forced dependency, self-esteem verges on the impossible, and self-hatred flourishes. In this situation accepting contempt and humility only deepens the demonic enslavement. What is first needed is a resurrection of love, self-esteem, and personal giftedness. Injustice in our world requires a correction and an adjustment of the wording of the Two Standards. For example, for someone trapped in servile dependency, assertiveness may initiate the development of the mentality of Christ, not of Satan. The danger of pride cannot deprive you of the essential human foundation of love and self-esteem.

Your appreciation of the standard of Satan, therefore, must relate carefully to human development without completely selling out to it. Human identity and maturity involve an experience of autonomy and of taking charge of one's own life, but not as one's ultimate goal. We all have a healthy need for affirmation. We seek this inner self-confidence to recognize the affirmation that God sends through other people. To a certain degree, as a healthy mature human being, you are the meaning of your own life—but you are never the *ultimate* meaning of your life. God is—and that is the standard of Christ. These nuances of the spiritual ideal of the Two Standards are very important today. Yet any misstep in distinguishing these nuances can have dangerous results spiritually.

All this, as presented in the *Exercises,* can seem like a quaint piece of folklore, worthy of a cynical smile on the face of a sophisticated contemporary person. But the person who laughs at the humor of C. S. Lewis's *The Screwtape Letters* (a satirical correspondence containing advice from a senior devil to a novice) without also shuddering in fear is blind to the serious challenge Lewis describes at the heart of human living. A blasé unbelief in the face of the enemy of our human nature takes the deadly sting out of Ignatius's caution and provides free play for the wiles of that enemy.

Ignatius's military imagery in the Two Standards can be replaced by other images. But to lose the image of warfare is to miss the central point of this exercise: a cosmic conflict touches us all. To deny the battle at the heart of human existence leaves you vulnerable, unprotected, without armor before the subtle yet deadly assault of the enemy. Paul's letter to the Ephesians (6:10–12) describes the battle and the armor needed: "Put God's armor on so as to be able to resist the devil's tactics. For it is not against human enemies that we have to struggle, but against the Sovereignties and the Powers who originate the darkness in this world, the spiritual army of evil in the heavens."

This lengthy treatment of the mentality of Satan lays out the framework and prepares for a view of the much more important and more attractive mentality of Christ.

The Mentality of Christ

Diametrically opposed to the satanic mentality, Christ's attitude of heart is the way to true life, now and into eternity. However, the attractiveness of his way is not immediately apparent. Only serious reflection, honest prayer, and continued begging for the grace of this meditation can reveal it.

Christ's recruiting tactics begin with a desire for spiritual poverty. This takes us back to Manresa, where in the depths of his helplessness Ignatius found a love he did not have to work hard to earn, a love he could hang on to, a forgiveness that rescued him. He learned that no human helplessness could ever conceal Jesus' loving presence. He learned to rely on him everywhere, for everything. This evangelical spiritual poverty is rooted in the nature of the human condition.

The message of human living is simple: you are helpless, unable to control even your own breathing. It is easy to assume the disguise of autonomy, trying to run your own life and wearing the mask of one in charge. But Christ's way is to embrace, not escape, the dependent vulnerability and find buried there the treasure of universal giftedness. A loving gift giver is blessing you in kindness beyond imagining.

This total dependence on God does not produce an immature passivity. The realization that you are nothing on your own, rather than deflating your spirit, stretches your heart. You wait in hope and gratitude for all the other gifts that accompany life. Everything about you belongs to God. Your stance in daily life is to welcome the Divine Majesty. Ignatius also suggests that you watch for the way the Divine Majesty will actualize your spiritual poverty in a simplified lifestyle. How different this mentality is from the previous one! The whole aura and aroma of it are different.

This stance in life is countercultural. Jesus is not just nice, neat, cool, fitting in easily with all culture. To follow in his way, sharing his mentality, bucks against most of our culture's traffic. Crossing the grain of the culture's moving traffic brings the collision of insult, ridicule, criticism, and contempt. Jesus had these reactions cast in his face frequently. It caused him suffering throughout his life and finally led him to his passion and death. The downward mobility of service in a culture competitively pushing and shoving in an upward mobility provokes misunderstanding, challenge, cynicism, or the put-down of simple disregard. In the face of this misunderstanding and ridicule, the foundation of God's intimate understanding and love, while it does not completely blunt these stinging reactions, does provide an inner balm and strength to stand firm and go on. Ridicule and misunderstanding often imply rejection, which is painful and stirs suffering in us all—as it did for Jesus in his humanity. These negative reactions will not utterly destroy you and your self-confidence if your experience of the understanding and affirmation of God's love in Christ is lively enough to stretch the sails of your heart.

To live daily in the awareness that all is gift describes a humility that is only possible because God has promised always to love and understand you. This takes the eyes of your heart off yourself. Louis Evely describes humility this way: "In a deeper sense, humility is a consequence of love: it is to cease to attach importance to oneself, because one so loves and admires another. It is to be not self-satisfied; it is not to worry about one's glory. . . . It is to put one's delight so much in another that one no longer thinks of oneself."[5]

A simple contrast between pride and humility does not capture the richness of this meditation. It takes four hours of serious consideration and prayer to find a direction in your heart's desire for the way of Jesus. These hours of prayer will give valuable insight not only into your own inner dynamics but also into the attitudes and vision implied in organizations and systems of our international world.

The Triple Colloquy

Each exercise has its own development from the grace desired that initiates the prayer to the colloquy that concludes it. In the Two Standards, meditation progresses from the graced enlightenment and courage begged for, through serious pondering and honest praying about the subtle dynamics of the two mentalities, to a true, realistic desire to walk the way of Jesus.

This desire to be received under the standard of Christ is the heart of the Triple Colloquy. Remember that a colloquy is a personal conversation, as between two friends.[6] Here the friends are Mary, the mother of Jesus; Jesus himself; and his beloved Father. You are to speak with Mary about your desire to be accepted in her Son's way of spiritual, and even actual, poverty and about bearing the reproaches and injuries that will come in whatever way the Divine Majesty determines for you. The project is God's, not yours. After beseeching Mary's intercession with her Son and his Father, you are to converse with Jesus and then directly with his Father, the Divine Majesty, about your desire to be part of the adventure of Christ.

This colloquy harks back to Ignatius's own experience walking with Favre and Laynez from Vicenza to Rome. On that walk he begged the Blessed Mother to place him with her Son. Then, in mid-November 1537, while resting in a wayside chapel at La Storta outside Rome, Ignatius had his second major mystical experience. He saw the Father and Jesus carrying his cross; their words made it clear that what he most desired had been granted: he was placed with Jesus in the ongoing struggle of salvation and glorification in our world. This experience thrilled his heart in unfurled desire; it also quieted, almost mesmerized, him for a while, and then always motivated his pilgrim life.

This experience at La Storta lies behind your own threefold conversation as this important day of prayer draws to a close. Ignatius summarizes the standard of Christ as the heart of this triple conversation. However, the exact words and fervor of the request will come from your own heart. The personal illumination from this meditation becomes the backdrop as you continue contemplating the mysteries of Christ. You are advised to keep the triple conversation in use as you move through the rest of the retreat. Over the hours this important meditation may have simplified for you into a desire for Jesus, for his way in your heart. Your desire to be with him, in him, clinging for dear life, can take on a contemplative simplicity and intensity. It seems no mistake that Ignatius, usually careful about words, refers to the Two Standards as a contemplation after its four hours of prayer.[7] He is very clear that the four hours on the Two Standards should be followed by another of his special meditations, the meditation on the Three Classes of Persons. In the next chapter we will see why.

8

Choosing and Loving Always for God's Glory

The Two Standards meditation is personal, decisive, and confrontational. It sets off fireworks as it challenges natural attachments you may have lived with for a long time, such as being honored or enjoying a comfortable life. Though the meditation on the Two Standards concludes with your honest, courageous desire for Jesus' mentality, those noisy attachments are stirring in the background, scheming to overturn any movement that might eliminate them.

Once again you face the problem of being faithful. How can you put into practice your genuine desire for the way of Jesus? Why does your desire seem to fritter away in the face of the first serious challenge? What about those natural attachments and addictions still stirring in your heart? The problem here is real. These natural feelings and sensual affections are not sins. But the questions they pose can assault the goal of living out your graced desire for the mentality of Jesus. Help is provided in Ignatius's meditation on the Three Classes of Persons. This meditation serves as an application of senses in dealing with those sensual attachments that are lurking in the shadows, ready to prey on your graced desire. All through this Second Week Ignatius recommends that the final hour of prayer each day be an application of senses to whatever sensual details of the mystery have come alive for you. So the meditation on the Three Classes of Persons in its own way responds to that recommendation and serves the need now stirring in your heart.

This meditation tests the durability of your graced desire for the standard of Christ. It addresses the cost involved when we always "ask for the grace to choose that which is more to the glory of the Divine Majesty and the salvation of [our] soul."[1] This is the *magis* desire again, the desire for your own unique call and role in the glory of God's love. Choosing simply for the glory of the Divine Majesty and choosing that which is *more* for the Divine Majesty's glory are two different choices. The second involves a more precisely focused commitment. The difference involves discovering, living, and acting on your unique *magis* role in God's movement to loving glory. It is a testing of your graced desire for Christ's mentality because a desire that wilts in the heat of action is not dependable and, thus, not very real.

The Glory of God

The glory of God shines through both the Scriptures and Ignatius's *Exercises*. This glory is a fire of love dazzling in the heart of God and radiantly mirrored in all created beings. God's glory is not just a glow suspended over all reality; it lives in human beings. For this reason, in the human sanctity of growth in closeness to God and of approach to that fullness, darkness plays an important part. Even the slightest mirroring of that glory, however, attracts and uplifts our hearts.

It is a glow that gleams from your own life both when you choose and act in a noble, magnanimous fashion and when everything about you radiates your distinctive, special role and vocation as revealed by the Divine Majesty. A human life with a distinctive

quality of choosing and acting in accord with God's love reveals—
indeed *is*—the glory of God in our midst. This is the heart of the
magis, the grace that shines all through the *Exercises* and, in this
meditation, is tested and prepared.

The greater glory of God is not a quantitative amount accumu-
lating somewhere on this earth or in heaven. Nor is it a reality that
sets people in competitive opposition to one another. Exactly the
opposite! God's greater glory forges the whole human family into
a unity of love and service. It relates to the *magis* desire in each of
us to assume our unique role in the developing glorification of
love. A life that manifests this distinctive, special vocation: this is
God's greater glory in our midst. The more we seek and live this
unique vocation, the more we all are gathered together by the Holy
Spirit in a balanced unity of God's love.

Ignatius's painful struggles at Manresa purified in him an
awareness of God's greater glory. He had left Loyola on fire for
what we might call the "greatest glory" of God. This ideal played
right into his personality, as always "going all the way." Halfhearted
efforts made no sense to this fiery combatant; it was all or nothing.
He would make sure that *his* loving and doing great things for God
would surpass those of everybody else.

But as we have seen, his helpless quandary in a cave at Manresa
opened him to deeper dimensions of the mystery of God. He
learned to wait on the Divine Majesty, who was always leading him.
He also learned to trust in a unique role that God ordained for
him, Ignatius of Loyola. Now the fire in his heart was not flashing
dramatically across the sky of his life. Burn it did, but more
steadily, quietly, and faithfully. That heroic "all the way" spirit still
lived in his heart. But it was manifest now in a way that would bend
to a lifelong variety of God's invitations and light his way, and that
of many others, right into the white heat of the eternal flame of

love. His concern to be faithful to the Divine Majesty's unique, special way of guiding him focused him on the greater glory of God. God's greater glory was not a reality on which he tightly locked his hands. That glory was always growing, leading, inviting in this world. He finally realized that it was not something he himself heroically determined. No, it was a way of daily living that the Divine Majesty revealed step by step with an attractive fondness that his pilgrim soul found almost irresistible.

This *magis* desire, always focused on the greater glory of God, gives an intensity to a human heart. It is an intensity not found in less focused, less energized, more laid-back hearts. Fr. Michael Buckley, S.J., claims this intensity can be seen in people's presence and comes from "a concentration of energies and a seriousness of intention that bear on what they undertake."[2] Buckley applies to the *magis* some of James Dickey's description of Gerard Manley Hopkins's poetry, "whose wildness and swiftness is so disciplined that it can become a life that is 'a language worked for all it can give.'"[3] This description of the poetry of the Jesuit Hopkins concretizes the appearance and effect of the *magis* desire for God's greater glory: a life that is "a language worked for all it can give." Rather than the intensity of one compulsively headed for a nervous breakdown, this energetic readiness bespeaks a heart entranced and focused uniquely by God's glorious love. This is the *magis* at the heart of the *Exercises* as spotlighted here in the meditation on the Three Classes of Persons.

Meditation on the Three Classes of Persons

Ignatius invites you into a specific scenario in this meditation. Three types of people have come upon a large supply of money. They know they must make a decision about their ownership and retention of the money. Each wants to accept God's loving will regarding the money. However, each one also feels a strong attachment to it, and each sees all sorts of uses to which the money can be put. Each person, finally, comes to the decision with a different disposition of heart.

The grace sought here is to see concretely all that is involved in choosing what is more *(magis)* to the glory of the Divine Majesty. The meditation is about the process of your commitment and how natural attachments and addictions can erode its power. Thus, the primary concern is not with what decision is actually made; rather, the central issue is the way of approaching the decision. Ignatius asks you to "imagine [yourself] as standing before God and all his saints, that [you] may desire and know what will be more pleasing to the Divine Goodness."[4] This is not a great feat of imagination. It is your actual situation at this very moment. You live in the immediate presence of a Creator-God whose love gives you life and, as shared in its fullness with all the saints, turns them also in care toward you.

The first class of person feels the attachment to the money and wants to make the right decision, but nothing happens. Whether fear, laziness, or the busyness of life explains the procrastination, the decision that needs to be made is overlooked. In *Draw Me into Your Friendship,* a contemporary reading of the *Exercises,* David Fleming describes this person as "a lot of talk, but no action."[5] The good intentions never get planted in the earth of daily life.

The second class of person reacts in a different way. A decision needs to be made and is made. With a keen sense of the attachment flaring in his awareness, this person decides, but decides too quickly, impatiently, maneuvering God's will to canonize the attachment. This one is the bargainer who, "like the rich young ruler who asks Jesus what he must do to inherit eternal life," is ready "to do everything, but the one thing necessary."[6] However aware the person may be of the inner dynamics, this individual avoids making the precise decision that God is asking.

Neither of these first two persons makes the decision to do more to the glory of the Divine Majesty. The person of the third class will make that decision, but not in a way that is rushed. This person takes the time for prayer and serious consideration to come to a freedom that could find God as much in keeping as in relinquishing the money. Such freedom is born of some real combat with the strong natural attachment to the money. But more than strong willpower and teeth gritting is needed. To place yourself before Jesus on the cross, as at the end of the First Week, calls forth and renews a basic posture of abandonment and freedom in the realization of how loved and forgiven you are. As mentioned earlier (see chapter 4), this is the touchstone for all future discerned decisions.

This touchstone of freedom becomes part of your heart's desire for what is more in line with God's glory. This third person, in the grip of the natural attachment, knows that a good decision cannot be made until necessary steps are taken. This person renews the experience of God's immediately creative and forgiving love. From this renewed experience, together with some serious grappling with the two alternatives, comes a freedom of indifference about keeping or relinquishing the money. Now, poised in the balance of this freedom, the Divine Majesty's choice for greater glory can be recognized and welcomed. In this way the power of the addictive attachment is undercut, not easily but with graced decisive activity.

Ignatius does not say what decision the third person makes. However, it is clear that the inner attitude in this class of person is the only one of the three that corresponds to the greater glory of God. This is the choice more *(magis)* in accord with divine glory through the exercise of a unique, special God-given vocation. Relinquishing the money is clearly not presumed as the better choice. More important than the decision is the proper inner attitude of freedom.

This meditation will stretch your soul in a variety of ways depending on the attachments stirred by your experience of the Two Standards. You will feel at home in parts of the experience of all three of the persons. Finally, however, you will learn how to integrate two dimensions of yourself: the deepest desire of your heart and the sensually affective skin of your heart. On this skin natural affections stir, rustle, and can harden into addictions—but never beyond the freeing power of grace.[7]

Ignatius concludes with some practical advice from his own experience. The power of disordered attachments can be broken by praying against them. If you recognize a disordered attachment to many things, beg God to deprive you of these things—never as something forced but only as you choose for the greater glory of the Divine Majesty.

As you conclude this challenging and enlightening day of prayer, crosscurrents of winds are blowing, and your sails are fluttering; you continue to learn about your distinct, special response to Jesus' mentality and call. Sorting through what you feel, what you think, and what you desire can profitably be shared in the ongoing triple conversation with your three friends: Mary, Jesus, and his Father.

Three Ways of Humility and Love

On the fifth day of the Second Week, you will return to contemplating the mysteries of the life of Christ. After a full day of serious prayer with the mentalities of Satan and Christ, a filter has been inserted into your heart. A wise sensitivity to the subtle dynamics involved in discipleship and a courageous desire to follow Jesus whatever the cost will help you now to listen even more carefully to God's revelation of Jesus to you. As this revelation takes root in your heart, specific aspects begin to coalesce in the new self promised before Jesus on the cross. Thus your own unique way of participating in the greater glory of God continues to be revealed. The whole retreat is aimed at your distinctive way of living for the greater glory of God. The rest of the Second Week concentrates on the revelation of this much desired *magis* vocation.

On this fifth day Ignatius recommends that you seriously consider three ways of loving.[8] These ways enrich your experience of falling in love with Jesus, and they further orient you to the revelation of your unique way of embracing God's greater glory. Love is never static; lovers are either growing closer together or they are slipping apart. These three ways of loving illustrate love's process of becoming whom you love.

In the first type of loving, your eternal salvation is so important that no reward, however pleasurable and appealing, would ever entice you seriously to offend your Beloved. This amounts to loving someone so much that you would go to whatever trouble may be involved to respond to that person's explicitly stated desire. This is a serious commitment of love, only possible because of your special experience of the Beloved's love and care for you.

The second type of loving builds on the first. In this experience of love you have a sensitivity that helps you to read the implicit, unstated desires of the Beloved as well as an eagerness to do whatever is involved in responding to those desires. This degree of love goes beyond the first and presumes the freedom of indifference. No natural craving for wealth, honor, health, or a long life will distract you from your love for the Beloved.

The third type of loving moves to a class by itself. Here the desire to imitate has become an eagerness to become one with the Beloved. Your desire is to share the whole being and condition of the Beloved. You feel strangely discontented if your condition is easier when the condition of the Beloved is difficult. This loving leads to a desire for poverty with Christ over wealth, for contempt with the burdened Christ rather than honors. You desire to be regarded as a fool for Christ because this was his condition.[9]

This third way is the pinnacle of loving in the Exercises. The saints know this dynamic. Francis of Assisi gives an example of this third way of loving when he describes perfect joy in a dictation to Brother Leo:

> I return from Perugia and arrive here in the dead of night; and it is wintertime, muddy and so cold that icicles have formed on the edges of my habit and keep striking my legs, and blood flows from such wounds. And all covered with mud and cold, I come to the gate and after I have knocked and called for some time, a brother comes and asks: "Who are you?" I answer: "Brother Francis." And he says: "Go away; this is not a proper hour for going about; you may not come in." And when I insist, he answers: "Go away, you are a simple and a stupid person; we are so many and we have no need of you. You are certainly not coming to us at this hour!" And I stand again at the door and say: "For the love of God, take me in tonight." And he answers: "I will not. Go to the Crosiers' place and ask there." I tell you this: If I had patience and did

not become upset, there would be true joy in this
and true virtue and the salvation of the soul.[10]

In this third way of loving, the balance struck in the Foundation
has been replaced by an even greater love. The clarity of this third
way of loving must not be overlooked: poverty, contempt, foolishness are not chosen for themselves. The heart's desire is for the
Beloved. Contempt, ridicule, and misunderstanding are your Beloved's
condition, so in them and through them you are with the Beloved
in love.

This consideration of loving is meant to stir the desire of your
heart as the contemplations engage you more and more with Jesus.
Ignatius does not expect the third way of loving to be part of you
now. Nor is it to be achieved by your hard work. The three ways
are left to ferment in your mind, heart, and imagination. All three
of the ways, most especially the third, are the result of the Divine
Majesty's stirring. If this third way of loving grows in your life, it is
part of the Divine Majesty's choice of a unique version for you. In
this thrilling vision at the highest pinnacle of the Exercises, the
eyes of the heart are on the beauty of the Divine Majesty in Jesus,
even when scorned and rejected, not on a Herculean project of
your will.

Karl Rahner adds another aspect as he summarizes this third
degree of humility and loving: "At least in death, man is the poor-
est of all: empty, weak, and deprived of all the honors of this world.
This is truly the end of the line. And if this is so, then it seems that
the third degree of humility is a practicing anticipation of what
God gives each man to do: to die in Christ absolutely poor and
empty."[11]

"To die in Christ absolutely poor and empty": this is not
just biological death for each of us. Ignatius dares to raise the

possibility of this as a busy disciple's way of serving the Beloved day after day until the final eruption into eternal glory.

This third way of loving is not some severe, ascetic picture of individual holiness. It is the way love grows and desires to serve to the end. The exercises on the Two Standards and the Kingdom give the apostolic thrust to this third way of loving. For the energetic, active apostle, the Divine Majesty chooses a way of sharing Jesus' forsaken condition of suffering that is usually not public and dramatic but much more hidden and ordinary. For Ignatius the dramatic loving and suffering of the early months of Manresa contrast sharply with the inner, hidden sacrifice of praise always rising from the heart of this busy general superior of the new, rapidly growing Company of Jesus.

As you consider these three ways of loving, the sails of your soul are stretched taut once again in heady gusts, not to the point of tearing but with a flexibility and a slackening that awaits a thrust of wind for resolute direction and full operation.

God's Election of the *Magis* for You

The direction of your person depends upon the revelation of God's election for you. After the day of the Two Standards, you follow eight days of contemplating the mysteries of Christ's life. Three elements suffuse this period. First, intimate looking, intent gazing, and attentive silence engross you during the contemplations. Second, the objectivity of the message revealed in the life and mission of Christ must be fully welcomed in your heart. Third, the drama of the spirits stirred in your heart will require the art of discernment for appreciation and interpretation. These three elements will determine the work of you and your director during this part of the retreat.

The most important election that gives fundamental direction for you is that of a state of life.[12] The basic states of life are religious consecrated life, priesthood, marriage, and a dedicated lay life of permanent celibate chastity. These differ from a career. A state of life is permanent and, therefore, involves a more serious type of profession and commitment.[13] Permanent commitment results from an overwhelming experience of love and involves a gigantic act of trust in the love of the Beloved.

If you have not chosen a state of life yet, then the Exercises can be an ideal experience to aid in such an important decision. When your heart is properly ordered to God's creative love, it radiates clarity and freedom. Decisions are best made in this clarity. They often seem simply to happen, though they must always be acknowledged and confirmed in the consolation of God's love.

God's revelation of your chosen state of life serves as an anchor for future stability and as a rudder to hold direction. To receive from the Divine Majesty the state in life that is most conducive for you to God's glory is a gift beyond pricing. Your state in life is not the result of financial greed, lazy inheritance, sheer chance, or ambitious maneuvering. It is a choice made by God precisely for you, as revealed in your contemplation of the mystery of Christ. This is the *magis,* that specially unique sharing in God's greater glory, a vocation and role that fits nobody but you.

Your desire for this *magis* has been growing from the early days of the Foundation. Without your realizing it, the whole process has been pointing you toward this revelation. The end of the First Week restored the possibility of your being faithful in God's process of creative glorification. The Kingdom meditation stretched your generous soul to the possibility of a wiser, refined loving. The meditation on the Two Standards brought a rude awakening to your eyes: a cosmic conflict of Christ and Satan, with subtle dynamics that confront you very personally. In the exercise on the Three Classes of Persons, you felt the challenge of choosing as someone whose identity is focused and stretched to a uniqueness in God's greater glory. Finally, while contemplating God's love in Jesus, you saw that your love for Jesus could grow to a desire to identify with him in his way of contempt, insult, and foolishness. This whole development has made you specially sensitive so that your contemplations allow God to imprint on your heart a unique image of Jesus. This is the image that uniquely fits you and draws you into the depths of the mystery of Christ in our world today.

These special Ignatian exercises of the Second Week play an important role in the development of your generosity, preparing you for the Election. But these special meditations in themselves do not have the power to reveal the Election. The mystery of Christ in the Scriptures radiates God's power of saving revelation. The special Ignatian exercises carefully focus the lens of the *Exercises,* but the film is the mystery of Christ.

If you already have your state in life settled before you enter the Exercises, then two courses present themselves. First, you can renew and confirm the state in life previously elected. Such a confirmation, a loud *yes* from God, is a precious moment of intimate communication, however clear it may have seemed to you all along. Second, this time of special closeness to God can refine different aspects of your basic state in life. A change of ministry, renewed fervor, a change of prayer: these adaptations, and many others, can renew your present state of life.

The Election is not so much what you decide as it is a revelation you await. It comes from the Divine Majesty from above *(de arriba)*. Sometimes the revealed Election surfaces and is gradually filled out during the days of contemplative intimacy with Jesus. No formal method is needed. But in other situations the revelation does not just happen. Then you can be helped by a formal process.

Three Times of Election

Ignatius presents three times for good elections or choices. These are really conditions of heart as you approach a decision. The first time is a condition of clarity worked by God that is without doubt, or even the possibility of doubt. Once again no formal method is needed. How often this happens is the subject of much discussion; it is probably rather rare in its pure form. However, with varying degrees of clarity and alacrity, this does seem to happen to a fair number of people, bringing them peace and a certainty of God's illumination.

In the second time, the condition of heart is fluctuating spontaneously from side to side regarding the decision. Attraction is followed by repulsion. Contentment, fear, and disturbance intermingle. This calls for the sorting out of these spontaneous stirrings through the art of discernment of spirits.

The third time involves a condition of tranquillity in the heart. Here you are spontaneously moved neither for nor against the point of the Election. In this time Ignatius presents two methods. In the first method your mind, reasoning coolly in faith about the evidence, is led to a decision. A careful renewal of the touchstone freedom at the end of the First Week is the atmosphere within which this method breathes. After begging for enlightenment regarding what is uniquely for you in God's glory, you gather the advantages and disadvantages of both sides of the Election. Tallying up is a matter not just of numerical majority but of the more significant reasons on each side. When reason, guided by faith and free from the influence of sensual attachments, reveals the weightier alternative, then you find God's will of love in that. Finally, this decision revealed and reasoned to in faith must be decisively offered to God with a request for confirmation that this is the Election in line with the greater glory of divine love. Recognizing this confirmation *de arriba* is an important conclusion of this first method.

The third time also has a second method. This method is aimed at a use of your imagination influenced by grace. After renewing the basic touchstone freedom and begging for the influence of God's love *de arriba,* consider this Election from three perspectives: the advice you would give as best for the holiness of a friend, what you would wish to have done from the perspective of your deathbed, and what you would wish to have done at your judgment before God. These will reveal the Election that is more for God's glory in your case. In conclusion, as in the previous method, you devotedly and decisively offer the Election with a request for confirmation.

The Election is a time of very sensitive, personal communication between you and God. It is a dance of mutual cooperation between the Creator and a valued cocreator. It is based on a great act of faith that the Divine Majesty can, and does, communicate the greater glory in a unique vocation and role of service for love.[14]

This communication is not utterly subjective, because it happens within the objective revelation of the mystery of Christ both in the Scriptures and in the Spirit-guided development of that revelation. Nor is the Election some clear and certain formula. No method is foolproof. Within the realm of the objective revelation, an intimately unique communication in faith flows from the Divine Majesty to you. Your reading of the signs in deep faith is the important sensitivity of a partner synchronized in this dance of cocreation and revelation. Patiently to trust the guiding hand of God and to follow divine confirmation absorbs the dance into grateful, decisive, daily living of what has been revealed. It is gold purified in the fire and meant to glisten long into the future.

The Election does not automatically happen at any given moment in the Second Week or, for that matter, in the whole retreat. The Election can be prepared for and clarified by the retreat but not crystallize until after the conclusion of the retreat. Whenever the Election crystallizes, it is God's revelation of something new, precisely for you. For this reason you are to enter this revelation thoroughly, become it, and live it immediately. In Ignatius's ideal program for the Exercises, the Election is worked on from the fifth day until the end of the Second Week on the twelfth day. If your Election is revealed by the end of the Second Week, you will have the rest of the retreat to live this new self.

As your Election is revealed and embraced, whenever that may be, a steady strong wind unfurls the sails of your soul. An unambiguous direction has been set, and a magnificent balance of taut and supple sails assures a smooth glide in that direction, however tempest tossed the sea may become.

9

A Compassionate Joy
beyond Any Disappointment

The contemplations of the Second Week on the life of Jesus flow into those of the Third and Fourth Weeks on his suffering, death, and resurrection. Usually another repose day is scheduled after about twenty days of retreat. While providing some needed rest and relaxation, this repose is not meant to interrupt the loving relationship with Jesus that has formed over ten or more days of contemplative intimacy.

Deepening of the Mystery

In the Third and Fourth Weeks the mystery of God's love revealed in Jesus takes on a distinctive, even shocking, character. The mystery of the cross and Resurrection was a scandal for the early disciples; these were events utterly unnatural and unexpected. That mystery is still a scandal today, even though it founds a whole new vision and life for those who believe. The depths of the mystery go beyond superficial faith and cheap grace. In the face of the mystery of the cross, fear, shock, and unbelief will shake your soul.

The contemplations of the previous ten days have prepared you for this further step. Contemplation of the mysteries of

Christ creates a new way of seeing and being—the way of love. It brings to your eyes and to your discourse a reverence, a sensitivity that invites you to patience and gives you the ability to see beneath the surface. In this part of the Exercises, contemplation brings you into the profound truth of things as they are. The amazing victory of God in Jesus reveals the deepest reality of life, and contemplation, as a long, loving look at the real, leads you beyond superficial appearances.

Unity of the Paschal Mystery

Though the whole revelation of the mysteries of Jesus has an overarching integrity, his suffering and death into resurrection have a special coherence and unity. When separated, they can lead to immature versions of the Christian life. Often the mystery is divided into horrendous defeat and then glorious victory. Unifying these two aspects was a great challenge for the early believers. It was accomplished in the Gospel of John after many years of reflection by the early Christians. Jesus says as his passion begins, "Now the hour has come for the Son of Man to be glorified" (Jn 12:23).

The unity of this mystery is part of the grace given through these days of prayer. Any increase in appreciation of this intimate interrelationship that comes to you from these days of contemplation will have a practical effect on the way you view life. When emphasis on the Passion is out of balance with emphasis on the Resurrection, life tends to take on an overly serious, hard, grim tone. With disproportionate emphasis on the Resurrection, a superficial optimism fights a losing battle with the tragic misfortunes of life. Christian spirituality over the centuries has fluctuated between these excesses in a struggle for the integrated unity of the mystery.

In the ideal development of the Exercises, your Election would be settled at this point. However—and I cannot emphasize this enough—the Election happens in God's time, not Ignatius's. If the Election has occurred, you enter this part of the retreat with some distinct advantages and disadvantages. On the positive side you now have time to live your revealed unique role in God's glory through the remaining days of the retreat. This will provide helpful confirmation and further appreciation of who you are called to be.

But with your revealed Election in place, some dangers also confront you. You can slip into the notion that the most important part is over. Or you could be overly concerned about your recent Election of life. The temptation to control a gift from God will often surface in your heart and can become a major distraction to entering the mentality of Christ. In another way a "finished" Election can underscore the strong tendency in us all to domesticate the cross. Another part of the grace hoped for here is to pierce through this defensive complacency to a renewed appreciation of your redemption in Christ Jesus.

Appreciating the unity of the mystery of Jesus' death and resurrection can also provide an important apostolic vision for your daily life and service. Endemic to human life in our world are undeserved suffering and violent rage. At times it seems that life is bathed in suffering. Suffering can have a deadening impact on our hearts. Frustration and discouragement invite us to despair. Many generous apostles working in our unjust world know these dynamics. Without a paschal vision of Jesus' suffering and death into resurrection, persevering service tends to corrupt into disillusionment. Only a profound ongoing experience of the paschal mystery can provide hope, joy, and enthusiasm right in the midst of the entanglements and violence of our world. Prayer with the Third and Fourth Weeks of the Exercises renews and enlivens this important vision for serious apostolic service.

Confirmation

These two parts of the Exercises serve a confirmatory role in three different though related senses. First, the rightness of your revealed Election can be confirmed by having about ten days to live in this newly elected identity. In this way the inner spirit of Jesus in his suffering and death into resurrection confirms your own inner spirit in living your renewed version of God's greater glory.

Second, your contemplation of Jesus' suffering, death, and resurrection will confirm the mystery of God's loving salvation throughout the whole universe. When a Jewish human being, the one and only Son of God, with a heart as big as the whole universe, took upon himself the sin of the world, what happened to him? These two parts of the retreat answer that important question and thus confirm your realization of God's loving salvation. Your amazing journey from the infinite ingratitude of sin to an infinite gratitude in Christ is accomplished at the immense cost of God's horrendous death in Jesus. To enter deeply into this mystery confirms in your heart the powerful victorious love of God for you and for us all.

Third, the confirmation of God's loving plan for you in Christ also reveals your own unique sharing in the glory of his suffering. Your revealed Election identifies you in the suffering mystery of Jesus. The realization of this, and even a growing desire for it, confirm personally your special role in the whole mystery of God's saving love.

These three aspects of confirmation are not the fruits of a convincing argument. They are *seen* beyond appearances during your contemplation in Christ of the truth profoundly submerged in all of reality. In this way these confirmations come from your continuing to take God's revealed love very seriously, especially now in the deep darkness of an undeserved dying.

The Grace Desired in the Third Week

The grace of the Third Week is in a direct, continuing relationship to the Incarnation contemplation. The suffering and death of Jesus continue to incarnate the Trinitarian decision to work the salvation of the human family. Jesus' suffering and death are part of a great process of creative and saving love, and they lose their significance when extracted from that context. The grace prayed for in the Incarnation contemplation—a special interior knowing of Jesus that coalesces with loving and inspires following—still resonates here in the Third Week.

In a continuing eagerness to enter the heart and mentality of Jesus, you ask for sorrow, compassion, and confusion "because the Lord is going to his Passion for [your] sins."[1] The words of this grace duplicate some of the words of the First Week, but this is no return to the beginning. The graced sorrow and confusion here have a far greater intensity and intimacy because of all that has happened in the meantime. Most especially, the grace of falling in love with Jesus in the contemplations of ten days has made him much more endeared as the beloved of your heart. To see your beloved suffer for your sins and to enter his own sorrow and confusion at your sin brings a much stronger graced response in your heart. You are now way beyond the First Week.

In the second exercise the grace specifies the compassion requested. This grace pulls you into the inner suffering of Jesus: "sorrow with Christ in sorrow; a broken spirit with Christ so broken; tears; and interior suffering because of the great suffering which Christ endured for [you]."[2] The focus is not on your suffering but on that of your beloved. A great emptiness of self and ego is required if this grace is to be effective. Such a grace is never easy, especially in our twenty-first-century American culture of self-absorption. As you prepare to ask for the grace suggested, you should appreciate, as much as you can, what it is you are asking of God. The consolation you seek comes from entering the suffering of Jesus. This ability to get out of your own suffering and to enter his teaches a very important lesson: to enter the suffering of other people you must get free of the all-absorbing clutches of your own.

Your own suffering is nonetheless the birthplace for compassion. A human being devoid of suffering is also incapable of compassion. The experience of being loved in your suffering frees you from the trap of selfishness and opens the way for the healing touch of compassion. Therefore, the grace of this Third Week of personal intimacy with Jesus in his suffering for you has invaluable ministerial implications.

The grace of this Third Week involves a war against selfishness and a transcending of your ego. In his passion we see Jesus living the advice he gave his followers from the beginning. In watching him do this through the contemplations of the Second Week, you are prepared for his dramatic self-denial and ego transcendence in the Passion. You also come to realize that, through the taking up of the cross that he advised for his followers, he knew in a special way an intimate reliance on and union with the One he called "my dearly beloved Father."

This grace of the Third Week is in many ways an uncomfortable grace. Watching your beloved willingly suffer because of your wrongdoing pierces the heart and brings tears. The mystery observed and experienced here is profound. Jesus suffered and died for our sins. That is the mystery, and it gives all reality a new life.

Trinitarian Experience of the Passion

From the beginning of the Second Week, you have been contemplating the Holy Trinity in their mission of salvation for us all. Here in the Third Week this perspective is crucial. The Passion is not just something that happened to Jesus. Its foundation lies deep in the loving heart of the Trinity.

Externally it is a series of cruel, undeserved events visited on the most innocent human being ever to walk this planet. The type of suffering and humiliation that Jesus endured for almost twenty hours repulses the imagination. This good, honest, forthright man is terribly abused and exploited. The physical external suffering should not be downplayed. But, all by itself, it is not the heart of the matter.

Internally the Passion plays itself out in the Trinity. The horrendous suffering has no simple and easy explanation. But in the heart of Jesus, laboring through his passion, you will discover a Beloved, dear beyond all and without whom he would have crumbled and broken. It was the support, encouragement, and presence of that Beloved all through his life that brought Jesus to this juncture and now kept him going, even in a moment when he was forsaken. Perhaps for the first time in his human life, Jesus felt bereft of the presence of that Beloved. Beyond what he was feeling in that moment of dire challenge, he believed, as always, in the presence of the One whose love was his very being.

The challenge of the contemplation is to pierce through the external into the internal Passion and to integrate these two dimensions in faith. Ignatius informs us that the divinity of Jesus is hidden in this terrible suffering.[3] He does not look very divine. But it is crucial for you in your contemplation to wait on the Spirit's revelation and thus find the hidden divinity. Otherwise, you have simply a man taken advantage of who does not resist. The Trinitarian dimension keeps the Third Week oriented to the Incarnation, where the whole Trinity willed your salvation by sending the Son as a human being. Though Jesus is understandably frightened, even dismayed, by the future suffering unto death, at the level of deepest desire in his heart he never wishes to escape this mission. He and his Beloved, inextricably united in the love of the Spirit, are always set together on your salvation.

The passion of Jesus, viewed internally in the Third Week, also figured in your First Week experience. In fact, that week concluded before Jesus on the cross as your savior, the one who courageously rescued you from your helpless, inescapable situation. These two experiences of the cross in the First and Third Weeks are both powerful and transforming, but they differ in perspective.

In the First Week the cross is the victory accomplished in Jesus, and you are the beneficiary. With great gratitude you know that you must live for Jesus. Paul's words in 1 Corinthians (15:17–20) describe this experience: "If Christ has not been raised, you are still in your sins. . . . If our hope in Christ has been for this life only, we are the most unfortunate of all people. But Christ has in fact been raised from the dead."

In this Third Week your experience of God's victory in Jesus has an internal impact of transformation. Your gratitude for being rescued in your helplessness escalates to another level. Now you desire to share the inner condition of Jesus' heart: both his suffering of scorn and within it his intimacy in faith with the Beloved. This is Paul's perspective in his letter to the Philippians (3:10): "All I want is to know Christ and the power of his resurrection and to share his sufferings by reproducing the pattern of his death."

The difference between these two experiences of the cross depends upon the third way of loving—a desire to share Jesus' poverty and humiliation. Obviously, this distinction is meant not to make your prayer here in the Third Week self-conscious but to enlighten your appreciation of God's love, drawing you ever closer into the mission of Jesus.

As this Third Week concludes, you must stay on Calvary long enough to be drawn contemplatively into what is really happening behind the external appearances. This takes time and is not always appealing, but one of the great gifts of contemplation is to help you to find the beautiful within what appears so ugly. The fifty-third chapter of Isaiah (verses 2–5) exemplifies this: "Without beauty, without majesty (we saw him), no looks to attract our eyes; a thing despised and rejected by men, a man of sorrows and familiar with suffering, a man to make people screen their faces; he was despised and we took no account of him. And yet ours were the sufferings he bore, ours the sorrows he carried. . . . he was pierced through for our faults, crushed for our sins."

Finally, you must let him breathe his last and be gone. You must walk around in the hollowness of this loss. The Resurrection is no miraculous afterthought. It grows from a tree planted on Calvary. To see the light dawning on the horizon of a sky marked by three crosses gives intimations of victory, glory, peace. The Pietà's image of a faithful mother treasuring in her grief the broken body of her son provides transition and gives birth to a hope, fragile and yet sturdy enough for victory.

As you come to the end of this Third Week, you have pierced through the dreadful, repulsive agony to something majestic and stately: a dignity, a nobility that stands faithful. The sails are slack now, but an indomitable wind begins to rustle and will not be restrained.

The Fourth Week

The Third Week, concluding in the pregnant lull after Jesus' death, catapults into the Fourth Week. The Resurrection does not correct the "mistake" of the Passion. The Passion is the other side of God's glorious love permeating the universe. It is a compassionate joy beyond any disappointment—something accomplished by the risen Jesus and also a way of life for his followers. You will come up with many apparent reasons for a lack of joy and hope, but in the end joy and hope are always possible in deep faith, born of the amazing victory that God has accomplished in Jesus.

That is why the contemplations continue to focus personally on Jesus, not on some abstract inquiry about the Resurrection. You have been encountering the risen Jesus all through the Exercises. Now, in his risen glory, Jesus reveals the fullness of the mystery of God's love—something not yet seen in the days of the retreat. Jesus' words at the Last Supper, "To have seen me is to have seen the Father" (Jn 14:9), are even more applicable here.

If the intensity of the retreat has left you fatigued, you may want to rearrange your schedule to get some rest. You may also take a mini-repose between the Third and Fourth Weeks, being careful not to interrupt their unity. Ignatius recommends four instead of five times of prayer and greater freedom for the spontaneity of the Holy Spirit's leading. Despite the freedom to appreciate your new life with the risen Jesus, this Fourth Week is not spent simply walking around in a heavenly daze. However rearranged your timetable may be, you need to pursue a schedule of formal prayer to continue your contemplative journey with Jesus.

This week begins with your own personal discovery that Jesus is risen. After the death and loss of Jesus, you must now wait and watch for his risen appearance within the framework of the month-long spiritual experience of prayer. This appearance cannot be forced and can happen in unexpected ways: at an early morning sunrise, while walking, at breakfast, while praying. Whatever the setting and timing, the experience touches your heart in faith with Jesus' wonderful assurance, "I have risen and am still with you!" The expectation of this personal experience should not be forced into something unduly extraordinary. But it should be patiently awaited and faithfully, reverently, wonderfully welcomed.

The Grace Desired in the Fourth Week

"To be glad and to rejoice intensely" is the keynote of this Ignatian grace.[4] Gladness and joy seem easy graces because our hearts yearn so much for them. But the grace here is not easy because it involves a persistent emptying of self. The motive for joy here springs from a desire to be identified with the Beloved, as in the third way of loving. Your gladness and joy are "because of the great glory and joy of Christ our Lord."[5] The spotlight is not on your joy and gladness but on his. Your joy shines forth from the sparkle of his.

As with the grace of the Third Week, you must transcend your selfish yearning for joy and enter Jesus' joy. This is not easy. Usually we feel more needed when a friend is suffering than when that person is glad and happy. But the grace requested here is to linger with Jesus in his joy. We want this selfless joy and gladness to take root deeply enough to become a daily experience.

The "intensity" of your rejoicing should not mislead you into an excessive expectation. Ignatius says that the divinity of Jesus, hidden in the Passion, "now appears and manifests itself so miraculously in this holy Resurrection, through its true and most holy effects."[6] Yes, the divinity is manifest, but the effects often take ordinary human expression. Contemplative faith, here in the Fourth Week and in daily life after retreat, helps you to find the extraordinary divinity of Jesus in very ordinary human interactions. Finding the extraordinary in the ordinary is part of the Fourth Week grace, initiated by your searching for and finding the hidden divinity of Jesus in his suffering.

The Risen Appearances

All the Gospels conclude with some appearances of the risen Jesus. Often we do not take them seriously enough because they seem like elusive stories. However, the fullness of the mystery of the Trinity's love shines forth in each of these appearances. The point of these encounters is not simply to prove the Resurrection. Rather, Jesus' many appearances help the early followers to believe that the unexpected has happened: Jesus is alive and present with them. These encounters help them become sensitive to his new presence among them. Life is different now. In these contemplations you too will realize and familiarize yourself with his new presence.

The first appearance Ignatius presents for your contemplation is not contained in the Scriptures.[7] The appearance to his mother is more than some sweet scene of filial piety; it is due to her giftedness. Jesus came to draw her into his joy. His joy is not something merely psychological. It is not simply that of someone dead who now is breathing again, nor is it the joy of an ambassador whose mission is successfully completed. Because his heart has been bursting with an infinity of love for us, the risen Jesus is flooded with joy because his love can be received again. The person who can most fully receive all that love is a woman, Mary of Nazareth. An amazing gift of sensitivity focused her life, not always in easy enjoyment, on her son. Far beyond filial piety, this encounter and sharing canonizes her as image and model of the whole church.

The risen Jesus always comes to console his followers.[8] For Ignatius consolation is much more than a matter of cheering up someone. It involves calling that person again to the glorious vision glowing in the heart of the Trinity, a vision that had been lost and buried at Jesus' death. The consolation of the risen Jesus reignites the fire of mission in the weak, embarrassed, timid hearts of his betrayer-disciples.

A dead man, now bursting with life and love, comes to console in a manner uniquely fitted to each follower. This is as astonishing for you as it was for the early followers in the Near East in the middle of the first century. It was a great challenge for them to relate this astonishing fact to Jesus' degrading, humiliating agony and death. But the wind of the Spirit blew the warm coals into flame. A wildfire grew and spread throughout the world and throughout the centuries, down to you today in this retreat.

The Trinitarian perspective remains intact in Jesus' appearances. At the heart of every appearance is the Trinity missioning the risen Jesus in an encounter uniquely fit to each person. You need to kneel in prayerful amazement before the Trinity still revealing a glory of love, expansive to the ends of the universe through all ages, and a uniquely special *(magis)* for every human being.

Contemplation will bring you inside the details, which will seem arbitrary and conflicting without it.

In each contemplation you will become aware of both the Trinity missioning in love and the Holy Spirit's detailed filling out of the scene. The full image and revelation of God in the risen Jesus radiates and marks your soul. The details of these encounters reveal how the risen Jesus is faithfully caring in ways that are charming, gracious, and humorous, even as he challenges unbelief. Through these appearances the early followers learned, and you will learn, that being risen does not remove Jesus but makes him even more personally present in the Spirit, a companion on the pilgrimage of life.

The careful contemplation of these appearances sensitizes your faith. It will help you to recognize in the daily details of life how the risen Jesus always comes to console you and then to mission you in consolation of many others. Another recognition also surprises you: the risen Jesus was consoling you every step of the pilgrimage of this month. You read the details of this ongoing appearance in the "gospel" of your own journal. Now you will be able to deal with the ordinary consolations and desolations of your inner life with a humble confidence, rooted first in your experience of the personal presence of the risen Jesus and then in the promise that he is of a joy and a victory beyond disappointment and defeat.[9]

Much has been revealed and learned in these Third and Fourth Weeks that you can profitably share in your continuing conversation with your three friends: Mary, the risen Jesus, and his beloved Father. These two weeks never end; they fuse into a daily way of living mirrored in the concluding exercise, the Contemplation to Attain Love, which is a summary of the whole retreat. These final days personalize your feel for finding God in all things and give you a humble confidence and flaming desire to live this new life.

Your desire to be faithful calls you to a faithful God who provides the way of your faithfulness. Your desire for this new life stretches your soul in faith and hope before the risen Jesus. He is God's invitation to your own unique role of serving in the endless sweep of divine glory. However, your confidence is humble because your own grasp on all of this is frail and fragile. Your hope and confidence are anchored in God's faithful loving grasp on you in the risen Jesus.

An experienced steersman has poised in a balance, magnificent to behold, the stretched sails of your soul, bracing and bending with the wind, and has readied you to cut through choppy surface waves to a sure destination.

10

Daily Life:
Gratefully Serving God in All

The *Spiritual Exercises* concludes with the Contemplation to Attain Love. This closing contemplation summarizes the whole experience of the retreat in a vision for daily living. Each of the points in this contemplation can be the material for prayer during the final few days. They can also be used as you leave the place of retreat and return home, bridging this experience with the rest of your life.

Sometimes at the end of the retreat people talk about returning to "real life." This makes the Exercises sound like an escape, an idyllic experience separated from the harsh realities of daily life. However, you have discovered on retreat a vision of the truth, about yourself and about all of life. Of course the external scaffolding of schedule, silence, daily direction, and the place of the retreat will come to an end. But the renovated structure of a new vision of heart now stands forth and becomes your life. Sorting out the elements of scaffolding to be disassembled from the renovated reality that can now stand on its own and must endure: this is part of your reflection on the closing days of the formal retreat.

Doubts about the sustainability of your experience will appear. These should be confronted head-on, seen for what they are, and held up before the great fidelity of God promised in the risen

133

Jesus. Otherwise, they will sabotage your experience. The enemy will always try to mislead you, but the power of God's desire for you in the risen Jesus is always greater than the machinations of the enemy. You must keep your new wits about you, recognize the temptations, and counteract them in humbly courageous faith. This will be an important part of daily life for you from now on.

The name of this concluding contemplation—"Contemplation to Attain Love"—is also instructive. God's love is to be *attained*, not *obtained*. It is not like a set of luggage, to be received and carried away at the end of the retreat! To attain something is to focus your mind and heart upon it. The greater glory of God's love, while surely an ontological reality in the being of God, is also a good-quality way of human decision making and living. That way of living attains and radiates the greater glory of God.

Some people have suggested renaming this contemplation "Loving the Way God Does." The whole retreat has drawn you into God's way of loving. Now, empowered and transformed by grace, you are missioned to love the way God does in your own unique *magis* role.

The Heart of Ignatius's Mysticism

In the synthesis for daily life presented in this contemplation, we see concretely a picture of Ignatius's vision of life. His religious ideal was to find God in all things and live the *magis* in the greater glory of God. The ideal is not the happy-go-lucky romantic *caballero* or the self-initiated, aggressive achiever eager to surpass all others. Nor is it the grim, seriously intent laborer. It is not ecstasy and rapture, the dramatic phenomena of mysticism.

Yet Ignatius had a great gift for mystical experience. The Cardoner enlightenment and the La Storta vision are his best-known mystical experiences, but his *Spiritual Journal* describes others.[1] These experiences, as extraordinary as they are, form part of his early mystical journey.[2] Later in life, during his years in Rome as general superior of the new Jesuit order from 1540 to 1556, his heart was stretched to the whole world. One can imagine that this man who had walked over most of western Europe would have loved to be trekking with Xavier in the East. However, it was clear to Ignatius that God's will for him was to stay in Rome, for the most part in three little rooms, prayerfully writing the *Constitutions* of this new order and serving as a center of communication and organization in its quickly developing mission. To be anyplace else would be to resist the *magis* of God's uniquely chosen glory for him.

The heart of mysticism is always an extraordinary gift from God, but the external expression of a mystical experience varies greatly. For Ignatius the external expression is as ordinary as hard work faithful to the task. The hidden motive of such work, of such service, is the extraordinary inner experience of a mystic: God's ravishing love vibrating in a zealous gratitude.

For Ignatius the extraordinary inner experience of divine love stretches the mystic to a pilgrimage for service in specific details of time and place. The incendiary power within the service is a gratitude—reverent, gracious, faithful—as in the risen Jesus, himself missioned to service from the heart of the Trinity. To love as God loves: it is the invitation of Ignatius because, first of all, it is the invitation of God in the risen Jesus. Therefore, the religious experience at the heart of Ignatian spirituality is a pilgrim mysticism of service. This mysticism, because less obvious, is more easily overlooked and contains within itself a huge danger and challenge, as we will see later in this chapter.

Fr. James Brodrick, S.J., the English historian, describes the subtlety of Ignatian mysticism in these words:

> Utterance was never one of Ignatius's strong points. Basques are famous for their taciturnity and when they speak they do so right on, as plain, blunt men, unaddicted to rhetoric. Azpeitia and Ávila might have been in different hemispheres for any resemblance in power of self-expression between Ignatius and Teresa, though as mystics they were brother and sister.
>
> Using music as an illustration, we might say that Teresa was a master composer, developing her themes and conveying by sheer genius all the rich harmonies of her experience. The most that Ignatius could do, or indeed wanted to do, was to hum the bare melody of his. "One day," he says, "while he knelt on the steps of the monastery reciting the Hours of the Blessed Virgin, the eyes of his mind were opened and he saw the Most Holy Trinity as it were under the likeness of a triple plectrum or of three keys on an organ." No doubt whatever, that is what he did see, but would such a simple vision have caused him to weep uncontrollably out of sheer joy for the rest of the day, or have left so profound an impression that throughout his subsequent life "he was filled with warm devotion whenever he prayed to the Most Holy Trinity,"

unless it had been accompanied by a marvelous divine illumination of which he says nothing?

It is the same with his visions of Our Lord's Humanity, of Our Lady, of how the world was created, of the manner in which Our Lord is present in the Blessed Sacrament. So vivid and penetrating was his apprehension of these mysteries of faith that he said "even if Scripture had not taught them he would have been resolved to die for them after what he himself had seen," and that was all he could tell. Put beside St. John of the Cross or Teresa or Mother Mary of the Incarnation, he seems at first sight like a sparrow among nightingales, but deeper understanding reveals him as belonging absolutely to their company.[3]

The Grace Desired

The grace recommended is rich with various elements. But first, two prenotes (#230, #231) set the Ignatian scene.

Contemplation to Attain Love

Note. Two preliminary observations should be made.

First. Love ought to manifest itself more by deeds than by words.

Second. Love consists in a mutual communication between the two persons. That is, the one who loves gives and communicates to the beloved what

> he or she has, or a part of what one has or can have;
> and the beloved in return does the same to the
> lover. Thus, if the one has knowledge, one gives it
> to the other who does not; and similarly in regard
> to honors or riches. Each shares with the other.[4]

The simple truth of these prenotes should not mislead you. First, love manifests itself more in deeds than in words. This gives a practicality to Ignatian mysticism, a quality that can easily be mis-interpreted. It also distinguishes the Ignatian brand from more sensually expressed mysticism. Second, love consists in a drive toward mutual communication and sharing between lover and beloved. These two prenotes sum up the reverential intimacy of the Exercises, especially as expressed in the contemplations of the life, death, and rising of Jesus. In this way the prenotes also pro-vide the foundation for this final contemplation's missionary thrust: God in all things to be sought and found in a mutually shared loving presence.

Fundamentally, the grace desired is a matter of gratitude. But gratitude is always response. Therefore, the grace presumes an awareness of the gift of God's love. The new element in this grace is "in all things" (*en todo* in Spanish) without any exception. You are asking for a deeply personal, internal awareness of how gifted you are "in all things." It is a continuation of the graced personal knowledge of Jesus from the Incarnation all the way up to this point. The precise challenge in the grace begged for here is that the awareness of giftedness is not limited to your preferences but is stretched to all things, whatever the future may hold.

This grace brings an enormous trust in the faithfulness of God's love. It transforms life itself into gratitude, and this gratitude forges a lifestyle of service. In the statement of the grace, however, the most important focus is in the syntax of grammar: the direct object of the service is the Divine Majesty. This is no slip of a pious pen on the part of Ignatius. A busy disciple encounters many people in a great variety of situations, but the direct, immediate encounter is always with the Divine Majesty. The grammar of a mysticism of service stretches your soul in an awareness of the fidelity of God's loving service to you.

However, a challenge is hidden in this graced ideal. Though mysticism is never humanly generated but is always divine gift, the grace prayed for here typifies Ignatian active spirituality. The inner religious experience reveals the Divine Majesty as direct object both of the motivating gratitude and of the service itself.

The danger is in settling for the active life of service without the inner fire of love. You are not meant to cause your own religious experience or to judge that of others, but the danger here is subtle enough to require regular reflection on the experience of your heart, lest you slip into and settle for the easier external appearance without enough of the religious reality motivating it all. Gratitude, with a quiet religious glow to it and for which no service asked is too much, images the wholehearted ideal here. The challenge is to see God's hand in all things *(en todo)* without any exception.

Gratitude and selfish pride cannot coexist in your heart, though most of us attempt a compromise. Just as before in the grace of the Third and Fourth Weeks, what is prayed for here involves an ability to transcend your own concerns. Only in this way can you see the gift in all of life and compassionately, gratefully serve, in the needs of your neighbor, the Divine Majesty.

In his last sentence of the treatment of the Election at the end of the Second Week, Ignatius points to the issue of selflessness: "For everyone ought to reflect that in all spiritual matters, the more one divests oneself of self-love, self-will, and self-interests, the more

progress one will make."[5] This is the heart of religious experience
and of Ignatian servant mysticism, though, as mentioned in chapter 7, this must be carefully integrated with today's knowledge of
human development. You find God in all things only insofar as
your self is mortified in all things.

The slow death to self reveals the exciting beauty of the risen Jesus
in all things. It is not something achieved at the end of a retreat; we all
grow in this ideal till we die. But we have a clear and certain reminder
that the paschal mystery of Jesus' suffering and dying into resurrection is the paradigm for human existence. We understandably resist
being fitted to this paradigm; the self never dies easily. But the reward
for such death to self is a precious, much desired inheritance.

A Developing Composure

In this contemplation the composition describes Ignatius's view
of the human condition. As in the meditation on the Three Classes of
Persons, you are to see yourself "as standing before God our Lord, and
also before the angels and saints, who are interceding for [you]."[6]
God's immediately creative love and greater glory surround and
breathe life into you at every moment. Only within the careful embrace
of this love is the grace desired in this contemplation possible.

This composure, however, is a development over previous ones
in the Exercises. In the First Week the composition was "to see in
imagination and to consider [your] soul as imprisoned in this cor-
ruptible body, and [your] whole compound self as an exile in this
valley [of tears] among brute animals."[7] In the Incarnation, part of
the composition is to see with the Trinity how the people of the
world are "all going down into hell."[8] These partake of a dismal,
forlorn, pessimistic view of reality. At times they are cited as

describing Ignatius's too sober and somber view, or they are discounted as old-fashioned and out-of-date.

Ignatius's full view of the human condition is the composure described in this closing contemplation. The dazzling presence of God's creating love is the final development of the whole revelation of the Exercises. Unless you are able to identify in some way with the truth and reality of the previous two composures (without getting stuck in their particular images), you will not appreciate the decision of the Trinity lovingly to save you and stand by you forever. The whole experience of the Exercises has brought you to this realization: you are saved in Christ Jesus. More than optimistic, Ignatius's view of the human condition is shining in faith and hope, always rooted in God's faithful promise of the Spirit in the risen Jesus. But this closing portrait is always born of a grateful awareness of being saved in the reality of the two previous compositions.

Four Points, Four Weeks

In a now classic article, Michael Buckley, S.J., describes how each of the four points of this contemplation summarizes one of the Four Weeks.[9] "The *Contemplación*," Buckley writes, "brings the major strands of the Exercises into their synthesis in love by recapitulating their graces in a heightened form. . . . a summary in consciousness and affectivity of major consideration of the previous four weeks."[10] In addition to summarizing the Four Weeks, each of the four points moves powerfully in a similar dynamic. The central insight of the point and of the corresponding week, once it has been realized anew, stirs a response of offering in the prayer "Take, Lord, and receive."

The First Point. I will call back into my memory the gifts I have received—my creation, redemption, and other gifts particular to myself. I will ponder with deep affection how much God our Lord has done for me, and how much he has given me of what he possesses, and consequently how he, the same Lord, desires to give me even his very self, in accordance with his divine design.

Then I will reflect on myself, and consider what I on my part ought in all reason and justice to offer and give to the Divine Majesty, namely, all my possessions, and myself along with them. I will speak as one making an offering with deep affection, and say:

"Take, Lord, and receive all my liberty, my memory, my understanding, and all my will—all that I have and possess. You, Lord, have given all that to me. I now give it back to you, O Lord. All of it is yours. Dispose of it according to your will. Give me love of yourself along with your grace, for that is enough for me."[11]

The first point of this contemplation "moves from creation to redemption and expands these to all personal graces."[12] In reviewing your experience of God's redemption in the First Week, a rereading of your own journal may be very helpful. A written version of your self-offering at the end of the Foundation and at the end of the First Week before Jesus on the cross may prepare you to recognize an even greater offering stirring now in your heart: "Take, Lord, and receive all my liberty, my memory, my understanding, and all my will—all that I have and possess. You, Lord, have given all that to me. I now give it back to you, O Lord. All of it is yours. Dispose of it according to your will. Give me love of yourself along with your grace, for that is enough for me."[13]

This offering should be prayerfully parsed phrase by phrase so it may stretch the generosity of your heart. You are not giving up use of mind, memory, will, and freedom; rather, you are promising always to see them as gifts and to use them only as God, their true owner, desires. Just as God has given all to you, so you now desire to return all of yourself in love. A lack of sufficient regard for yourself reduces the offering to "good riddance" of what you yourself do not like; the hope is that any deficient view of self has been corrected through the Exercises. The frequent use of the word *all* throughout Ignatius's prayer keeps stretching your heart, both in realization of how loved you are and in your own responsive generosity.

> *The Second Point.* I will consider how God dwells in creatures; in the elements, giving them existence; in the plants, giving them life; in the animals, giving them sensation; in human beings, giving them intelligence; and finally, how in this way he dwells also in myself, giving me existence, life, sensation, and intelligence; and even further, making me his temple, since I am created as a likeness and image of the Divine Majesty. Then once again I will reflect on myself, in the manner described in the first point, or in any other way I feel to be better. This same procedure will be used in each of the following points.[14]

As Buckley's article notes, "The second point of the *Contemplación* considers how God does not remain outside of . . . creation, but dwells within creatures, affecting them to be what they are by this presence. . . . The Incarnation becomes the highest instance of presence, but it does not exhaust it."[15] That the Son is sent from the heart of the Trinity to become a human being is amazing in itself but has even more awesome implications. God does not gaze on creation from afar but is present in it. "God not only gives," Buckley writes, "but . . . lives within [the] gift. . . . Things are not only gifts, they are holy: for they contain God."[16] Once again your journal of your Second Week experience or the reflection on a specially graced Scripture passage about the Incarnation will stir your heart's experience of awe and wonder to love and gratitude.

> *The Third Point.* I will consider how God labors and works for me in all the creatures on the face of the earth; that is, he acts in the manner of one who is laboring. For example, he is working in the heavens, elements, plants, fruits, cattle, and all the rest—giving them their existence, conserving them, concurring with their vegetative and sensitive activities, and so forth. Then I will reflect on myself.[17]

The words *work* and *labor* (*trabajar* in Spanish) have a special resonance of application to the third week of the Exercises: Jesus labors through the sufferings of his passion, and you, the retreatant, labor through the points for prayer over the Passion. In this week "one contemplates Christ at what Ignatius called his labours, the greatest costs and suffering which the Kingdom forecast."[18] In the third point: "[A] theme of the third week is resumed . . . as the work of God in all things, the work of which the passion of Christ is paradigmatic, and in which all things . . . are seen as events and moments in which [God] labors. Again the internal development is obvious: God who gives, God who indwells—now God who works out the salvation of [people] within all things. And the concomitant growth in the vision of all things: first as gift, then as holy, now as saved history."[19]

This third point is also importantly Ignatian. The perception "that God works, labours in all things . . . struggles when the galaxies move, that the rush of life is indicative of his sacred toil, that all things are caught up in the redemptive workings of God . . . is not so common a tradition."[20] This uncommon insight of God as present and at work in all things is the foundation for discernment: "[The] attempt to read, to interpret and to understand things as caught up in [God's] labours and directions, bears upon any contemplative apostolic life. To do so in particular is religious discernment; to do so universally, to recognize in general what is taking place, is the vision of this [third] member of the *Contemplación*."[21] As this awareness of God's constant loving labor for you in all things dawns and is renewed, the lyrics echo again in your heart: "Take, Lord, and receive."

> *The Fourth Point.* I will consider how all good things and gifts descend from above; for example, my limited power from the Supreme and Infinite Power above; and so of justice, goodness, piety, mercy, and so forth—just as the rays come down from the sun, or the rains from their source. Then I will finish by reflecting on myself, as has been explained. I will conclude with a colloquy and an Our Father.[22]

The Fourth Week features the risen Jesus in the fullness of his victory and glory:

> In the fourth point, the *Contemplación* now moves from the acts of God to their source. . . . Everything speaks of God as it resembles him, and calls back to God as the image calls back to its reality. This is to catch some glimpse of Who is giving, Who is present, Who is working and labouring for [human beings]. The transition of this point is from the acts of God to the reality of God. . . . a shift made possible because things are not only gifts and holy and sacred history—they are participants in [God's] nature.[23]

Just as Ignatius learned to wait for revelation *de arriba* from the Divine Majesty, so the Exercises have readied you to recognize the risen Jesus sent from the Trinity. The mutual interior knowledge of Christ our Lord, prayed for from the beginning of the Second Week, climaxes now to a fullness of intimacy in the very depths of God, as revealed in the risen Jesus of the Fourth Week and synthesized here in the fourth point. This contemplation traces a maturation in your loving: from loving God because of what you received in Jesus, you have risen to a love for God more simple and pure, motivated by infinite beauty and goodness itself, blindingly radiant in the Trinity. This is an astonishing, bold final step on the part of Ignatius.

In conclusion and in summary, the *Contemplación* "resumes the principal themes of the four weeks of the Spiritual Exercises into a synthesis by which a person moves gradually to [the very heart of] God . . . to whom [the person] surrenders in all things."[24]

The Ignatian pilgrim mysticism of service finds God in all things by entering carefully into the tangled human situation rather than by withdrawing from it. The special contemplative nature of this experience makes the service always radically religious, however secular it may appear. This radically grateful, religious service can heal the sacred-secular split in your experience that often saps apostolic energy.

Finding God in all things is never produced by human effort, but it does require your cooperation in a number of specific attitudes and practices. Some of them are: (1) a belief that God is truly available in all things, (2) an ongoing experience of God's love as beyond all else and as enough in itself, (3) an asceticism of mortifying self in all things, (4) regular, formal contemplation that is more than a vague, casual reflectiveness, and (5) a careful monitoring in faith of the spontaneities of light and darkness in your heart. I call this "consciousness examen."[25]

For Ignatius the finding of God in all things through a mysticism of service happens in an ecclesial context. I will comment further on this presumed ecclesial context in the next chapter when I treat some of the rules found at the end of the *Exercises*.

Stretched for greater glory, aglitter in the sun and gracefully balanced in the crosscurrents, the sails of your soul now give a firmness and solidity of movement for cutting your way deeply and smoothly through the waters of life.

This chapter concludes my treatment of the dynamics involved in the formal experience of the Exercises. In the next three chapters I will treat material appended at the end of the *Exercises*. The explanation of the rules for discernment will reveal other dynamics that run through the whole experience both of the formal Exercises and of daily living in careful faith.

11

Methods of Praying
and Some Rules

In this chapter we will consider some material found at the end
of the *Exercises*. Ignatius presents three methods of praying and
sets of rules concerning eating, scruples, the distribution of alms, a
genuine attitude within the church, and discernment of spirits.
These units have different relationships to the full experience of
the Exercises; some are essential, while others could be bypassed
by some retreatants. For example, the rules for discernment, which
I will explain in chapters 12 and 13, are crucial in every experience
of the Exercises.

Three Methods of Praying

Thirty days of praying makes the Exercises a school of prayer.
During these days of retreat you have prayed more often and more
intensely than usual. By practicing the different forms of prayer
Ignatius recommended, you have learned a lot about your own
style of praying. The transition from this intense period of prayer
on retreat to more ordinary prayer as you return to busy daily life
becomes very important. What kind of gradual transition can you
make from the intensely personal prayer of retreat to the daily

prayer now submerged in a much more busy, active life? Can you maintain the affective intensity of your retreat prayer? What changes are you being asked to implement in your daily prayer? How can you avoid losing over time most of what your new experience of prayer has taught you? Questions of this sort highlight the importance of prayer as you leave the place of retreat.

The three methods of prayer, appended after the concluding Contemplation to Attain Love, are meant to help with the transition. Prenote #4 in the beginning of the *Exercises* informed you that these methods are part of the Fourth Week. However, a study of the wording of the first method puts it in a class by itself. If related at all to the full Exercises, it can be a type of long-range preparation, as in prenote #18. The other two methods, however, presume and follow a thirty-day retreat.

In the second method, you take a vocal prayer of the retreat that has been inflamed with special relish, and you rest in it, word by word. This could be done with psalms or other Scripture texts. Hours of this prayer of repetition over many days allow the thrust of intimately personal prayer, built up through the month, to flow into and fuse with the ordinary prayer of daily life. Your journal can serve as a reminder and invitation to those prayer passages still ringing with a special affective resonance for you.

In the third method, you take an affectively alive passage and fit your recitation of the words to your breathing. In this way you come to realize part of the great gift of this month: your breathing person is a praying person. Prayer has so deeply watered and sanctified your person that it easily spills over into words. Once again the affective resonance glows as the words walk in your speech and step off your tongue. This can make up a full hour of prayer or, more likely, serve as moments of recollection sprinkled throughout your busy day. Psalm 139 or the words between Jesus and Bartimaeus—"'What do you want me to do for you?' . . . 'Master, let me see again!'" (Mk 10:51)—or so many other possibilities are available to you for these two methods of praying as the end of the formal retreat quickly becomes busy life.

Expectations and desires play an important role in this transition. It is unrealistic to expect over time to feel the same emotional intensity of prayer that you felt in the structured prayer and solitude of your retreat, and the lessening of that intensity is not necessarily a sign of negligence. You have also learned a lot about your desires, which stirred within you as your response to the revelation of the mystery of Christ. These desires coalesce in a unique personal relationship with God focused in the risen Jesus, which becomes a foundation for every aspect of every day.

You must learn to take steps daily to keep this renewed relationship alive and personal. For example, any animated love relationship overflows into an awareness that keeps the beloved present with the lover. Your renewed awareness of how alive, present, and personal God's love is in Jesus brings awe and astonishment. Do what you can to prevent that awe and astonishment from lulling into complacency, but never forget: God's personal desire for you and your faithfulness far transcends your own desire. The risen Jesus is promise and proof of that.

Rules

Ignatius uses sets of rules to communicate simply and clearly his own experience. For the most part these are so bluntly stated that they can seem cold and impersonal. When they are separated from experience, both Ignatius's and your own, they are easily misunderstood.

Each one of the rules is meant as a commentary on your experience; each provides insight and balm when given to you while you are in the midst of the experience it describes.

The rules presume the contemplative attitude of the end of the retreat. The composure presumed in all the rules is that of the personal presence of the risen Jesus with us always, revealing the immediacy of God's creative love and the process of glorification simmering through the whole expanse of reality. To step outside that contemplative composure changes the focus of the rules and makes them difficult to appreciate.

The rules were assembled in the first half of the sixteenth century and therefore often require an application to our contemporary situation. In some cases this application is obvious, whereas in other cases it is anything but. Not all the rules are essential to a full experience of the Exercises. The rules for the discernment of spirits, "as reflective codifications of how Ignatius believed his own conversion had happened at the castle of Loyola and continued at Manresa, and of his pastoral experience since then . . . are at the very core of the *Spiritual Exercises*."[1] Some of the other rules may never come up during the month of retreat.

Rules for Scruples

These rules are drenched with Ignatius's own painful experience at Manresa. His soul-wrenching experience, described in his *Autobiography,* provides valuable background reading for these rules.[2] "Scruples" in these rules are spontaneous movements of spirit requiring the faith interpretation of discernment. This distinguishes them from another type of scruples, an emotional sickness. This sickness, often evidenced in a severe inability to trust that can interfere with the productivity of one's life, sometimes requires therapy. Ignatius is not chiefly concerned with this latter type. He applies the

criteria and principles of discernment to the scruples insofar as they
are spiritual movements and not evidence of emotional sickness.

In this sense scruples are seen as a part of a person's faith development. Sometimes a new, big step forward in faith maturity
results in a shiver in your affectivity. This type of scruple is part of
your heart's affectivity, worrying about the impending change and
whether an agreement is to be struck with your new, more mature,
faith sensitivity. The issue here is a growing wholeheartedness in
faith, always the goal of discernment. Proper discernment, therefore, is needed to recognize and respond to this invitation of God.
Either to treat this as emotional sickness or not to discern it properly would be misleading.

Rules for Distribution of Alms

Michael Ivens, S.J., places the rules for distribution of alms in the
important context of Ignatius's time when he says, "Composed
during Ignatius's Paris years, the Rules for Almsgiving deal with
some of the concrete implications of the reform and amendment of
life in the sixteenth-century church and society."[3] In assembling
these rules for serious consideration, whenever they are so needed,
Ignatius reveals his awareness of the corruption so widespread in
the church and society of his time.

The issue here is a matter of making a discerning election about
the alms to be distributed. An election made by flipping a coin or
influenced by a disordered natural attachment is not serious
enough and makes the giver part of the problem rather than part of
its solution. Ignatius makes explicit reference here to the material
about Election presented earlier in the book. In these rules he
shows his belief in the spiritual value of poverty and generosity in
the way of Jesus, as presented in the meditations and contemplations for the Second Week. These prayer experiences provide the

spiritual motivation for electing a distribution of alms in accord with spiritual poverty and the generous avoidance of any disordered attachment.

Rules for Eating

These rules are meant for someone in the full experience of the Exercises. Their position is a matter first of curiosity but finally of great importance. Why are they separated from the other rules at the end of the book? Fasting and penance, treated earlier in the *Exercises,*[4] are not the topics of these rules. You do not look to these rules for guidance about the practice of fasting during retreat. Though at first glance they seem out of place, their positioning between the Third and Fourth Weeks puts them exactly in the center of the paschal mystery of Jesus' suffering and dying into resurrection.

This placement makes all the difference. These rules describe how you would apply the vision of the paschal mystery to an area of human life as basic as eating. How does someone eat who has internalized Jesus' attitude in the paschal mystery? These rules cannot be fully understood until after you have contemplated the integral unity of the Third and Fourth Weeks. These rules concretize and particularize the paschal vision of Jesus in the area of eating. But the approach within these rules can, and usually should, be applied to other areas of human life, such as the use of TV, of the Internet, and of recreation, to name just a few examples. How would you live the wisdom and joy of Jesus' paschal mentality in these personal areas of daily life? These rules help you reach an inspired, concrete answer.

Finding God, and not self, in the use of food is a contemplative and discerning art. First of all, it does not mean that food cannot be enjoyed for itself. Joy in food and drink involves more than the sensual and the dietary and therefore opens up the possibility of finding God in your eating. Reflection on the experience of over-eating points up the issue. Besides being unhealthy and causing gastronomical discomfort, overeating obstructs the spiritual focus of your heart and blunts your sensitivity to God. To eat properly is to eat as one with the contemplative awareness of the loving personal presence of the risen Jesus. The application of senses can help you to enter sensually into the mentality with which Jesus eats.

Discovering the "right mean to keep for oneself in eating and drinking"[5] requires careful experimentation and discernment. This "right mean" is not some dietary, caloric average that one follows rigidly; it can be discerned properly to a different concrete conclusion for different people and in different situations. The goal is the spiritual health of eating and drinking in a way that reveals God's consolation and inspiration. The self-indulgence of overeating, on the other hand, suffocates this advantage.

These rules are open to many important applications. They can serve as a guide for discerning the situation of hunger and food distribution in our world.[6] In a culture and time of much over-eating, these rules provide a contemporary challenge. They can also provide a necessary spiritual balance in other areas of your life. Clearly, these rules play their own important role in the transition from retreat to daily life.

Rules for a Genuine Attitude within the Church

This concluding set of rules in the book was composed while Ignatius was at the University of Paris and completed after his arrival in Rome. They were composed by a man who, with his early companions, had only recently experienced the lies and slander leveled at them in Venice and Rome in the last half of the 1530s. Ignatius was a man thoroughly aware both of the serious abuses in the church at that time and of the urgent need for reform and renewal. His strong conviction, however, was for a reform from within the Catholic Church and not from an outside position after having stepped beyond the church's ranks. These details influence, and are manifest in, these rules.

We should not exaggerate the controversy these rules provoked in the church in Ignatius's time; O'Malley speaks of "the relatively little comment and controversy [they] aroused in the sixteenth century."[7] Since these rules were created by a man of the sixteenth century and intended for that particular time, their significance and application to contemporary times are not easily determined. But today, in a time and a church where polarized positions often encamp against one another, these rules stir more controversy. Ignatius did not resolve these oppositions, nor will I specify the modern application of these rules. How central are they to the Exercises? Could someone make the full retreat and not read these rules? Michael Ivens, S.J., tells us, "Certainly the Exercises cannot be made authentically except in a consciousness of the Church; but this need not always be the kind of consciousness required by the rules. This indeed is acknowledged in the *Directories,* which insist that the rules should be given not as a matter of course, but only to those who need them."[8]

Michael Buckley, S.J., in the "final word" of a very valuable paper on "Ecclesial Mysticism in the Spiritual Exercises," provides a direct, positive answer to this question: "What, then, is the place occupied by the hierarchical or institutional church in the *Spiritual Exercises?* It is the context and the paradigm for the immediate experience of God."[9]

The word *church* occurs very infrequently in the *Exercises.* But as a context, a consciousness, an attitude, "church" underlies the whole development. Ivens states that the "implicit ecclesiology of the Exercises, and indeed of the whole of Ignatian spirituality, is

developed by Hugo Rahner on the basis of the incarnational principle that 'spirit always tends towards flesh, and that the movement of God's spirit means incarnation and building up the body
of Christ.'"[10]

This subliminal importance, easily overlooked, is highlighted
in metaphors Ignatius uses for the church in these rules. Twice he
refers to the church as the spouse of Christ and as our mother.[11] In
all of his writings Ignatius very rarely used spousal imagery.
Though he was aware of and influenced by the use of these images
in Scripture and tradition, Ignatius's use of them here to refer to
the church is deliberate and significant. In a mysticism of service
the spousal relationship is not as central as it is in a mysticism of
union.[12] But the use twice of these images of spouse and mother for
the church highlights his central ecclesial consciousness in the
whole development of the *Exercises*. Buckley summarizes this central value as focused in the two images: "[The ecclesial metaphors]
illumine lines of argument or development within the progress of
the *Exercises*, indicating that the church possesses a profound
importance—a taken-for-granted importance—in the internal
structure of the *Exercises* as a whole. The world of the text comes
to a focus in these symbols, which occupy so slender a portion of
its pages."[13]

These images highlight the fact that these rules are primarily
concerned with a disposition and a sensitively discerning attitude.
The concern is not with specific theological positions to be held or
with particular actions to be done. Influencing all actions, words,
and gestures regarding the church is a special inner attitude: an
alert sensitivity to the guidance of the Holy Spirit of God at work
in the church.

The title of these rules is not easily shorthanded. "Rules of
Orthodoxy" and "Rules for Thinking with the Church" are

misleading because orthodoxy is not the prime concern and the attitude highlighted here involves more than thinking. The Spanish word translated as "attitude" in "Rules for a Genuine Attitude within the Church" is *sentido,* a key word in Ignatian discernment. The attitude presented is that of someone fully within the church, not someone looking at the church as an object from the outside. The preposition *within* catches this refinement. We, as any localized group of believers, never own the church, because the church is Christ's spouse. Yet, as people of God embracing a variety of roles of service, we all constitute the church.

An attitude of promptness and readiness is the grace prayed for in the Kingdom exercise. An eagerness for God's way revealed in the risen Jesus is sought in the church because the same spirit of love animates Christ and his spouse.[14] All through the Exercises the objective revelation of the mystery of Christ pointed the way for and fueled the retreatant's subjective experience. So in any Ignatian discernment, and especially here in the fundamental ecclesial attitude of the Exercises, the inner subjective sensitivity catches fire and is validated through integration with, and concrete particular expression of, the objective biblical, ecclesial revelation.

The intimately personal love you have for the risen Jesus spills over into a love for his spouse, the church. A similar personal love of commitment is involved in relating to the church as a dearly beloved mother. The *sentido* attitude expected here is neither overly intellectual nor overly emotional but integrates these two elements with all the other forces of a person in a deep-hearted, loving faith. An attitude like this may at times criticize, but always in a way that demonstrates beyond words a genuine, personal love for a mother and for a dear friend's spouse. Therefore, how, when, and where the criticism is given are never irrelevant details.

In all these rules Ignatius's style is not argumentative or polemical. He is offering calm, wise counsel. In line with this he urges praise, not necessarily personal practice, for lots of different devotions and actions.

Though these rules are not a set of specific orthodoxy norms, they focus in terms of the church the eagerly discerning attitude of faith, hope, and love that characterize the end of the *Exercises*. Buckley summarizes it this way: "It is important . . . to assert the critical position of the church in the *Exercises,* one which allows the *Exercises* to grow into their own promise as the church develops in its own self-understanding over the four centuries since their initial composition."[15]

12

Discernment of Spirits
in the Exercises

The experience of the Exercises is a school of discernment as well as of prayer. The two are always in close relationship. Because this school teaches us very personally about these two interrelated areas, an integrated practice of them is always the homework that follows any experience of the Exercises.

Because discernment is central to the Exercises, the collection of rules for the discernment of spirits in the back of the book is very important. The rules spark a number of reminders: This experience is not something you do to and for yourself. It does not leave you placid, untouched, unmoved; rather, it sets loose a swarm of spontaneous inner spirits. These rules help you to interpret and respond to this variety of spiritual movement. The rules are divided into two sets: the first introducing a beginning sensitivity and the second describing a more mature interpretation.

In this chapter, after some introductory reflections, I will comment on the first set of rules; I will discuss the second set of rules in the next chapter.

Introductory Distinctions

Discernment of spirits is the art of holiness for human beings.[1] This type of discernment has two foundations: God's revelation in Jesus and the human condition of your heart. When you listen seriously to Jesus in the Scriptures, you learn how personally God loves every human being and how challenged that love is by an admixture of evil throughout all of reality. At the same time, the human condition of your heart concretizes the revelation of Jesus in your experience of a mixture of spirits, both good and evil. This admixture of good and evil poses the critical issue of meaning and identity for us all. To recognize good and evil and then to act on that recognition is the heart of the matter. Though it sounds clear and logical, you know it is not easy and does not always turn out as you might wish.

In this sense discernment is the story, the only story, of human faith development. Ignatius has his own way of describing this story, while other traditions have different terminologies to articulate the process. But fundamentally, the process is the same. It does not belong to Ignatius or to any other human being. God composes and tells the story of holiness in the ongoing creation of our universe and of our human hearts. In Jesus, God also invites us to play a unique role in that story of holiness. I will be commenting on Ignatius's version as presented in the *Exercises,* but it is important to remember whose story it is from beginning to end. The initiative in holiness is always with God in the beauty of Jesus.

Every human heart houses a fluctuating conglomeration of impulses, moods, phantasms, feelings, daydreams, and more. The heart can be overwhelmed at times by the intensity and sheer diversity of it all. To move ahead requires a resolution of the intensity and the diversity. Petrified in the face of it all, you remain motionless, confused, and sometimes frustrated. The resolution that allows progress entails a careful sorting out and separating of these inner movements of your heart. And the basic dictionary meaning of the word *discernment* is just that: to sort out, to separate. So it is discernment of spirits, a sorting and separating out of inner experiences, that helps you to unlock the immobility and to move ahead in developing your true identity and the direction such identity gives for all the activity of life.

In the story of holiness, God intends for each of us a unique imitation of Jesus. Your true self is a glorious revelation, filled with promise for you and for many other people. This identity in faith, and this alone, will satisfy and fulfill the deepest yearning of your heart. It is the goal of all the searching in your life. If only it were a gift easily received, a reality delivered securely into your hands at a set time! But this true self, this unique imitation of Jesus intended for you by God, is a gift for which you must rummage all through life because this priceless gift is camouflaged within the conglomeration of spontaneous movements stirring in your heart.

As a result, from the spontaneous mixture of mood, impulse, feeling, and daydream, something intentional is born and assimilated into who you are. This intentional self, if chosen and discerned correctly, is your true self. But because of the present flawed condition of the human heart, the bright flower of your intentional true self may be concealed in an overgrowth of weeds and underbrush. In the treatment of the First Week in chapter 4, you waded into and exercised a discernment of a murky, darksome, frightening example of this overgrowth.

To back off, to hide from this troubling spontaneous part of yourself, is to bypass holiness and forfeit the gift of your true self. Holiness does not descend like a heavenly mist but is discovered through a careful sorting out of your inner spontaneous life. A decision to enter the fray and search for this holy grail brought you into the Exercises at the very beginning and kept you persevering faithfully. Your own motivation for the search is always buttressed by a much greater desire: God's intense desire in love for you every step of the search. The rules for discernment of spirits are concerned with this search and the sorting out of spontaneous spirits to reveal the treasure.

Three Dimensions of Human Living

The search for your own holy grail always brings you into the relationship of three different aspects of the self: external behavior, interior spontaneity, and what I call the "core of the soul." A proper relationship among these three elements of your humanity, focused in a lived integration, is the chief concern of faith maturity. When these three elements are properly integrated in faith, a hidden self grown strong is exposed, always aglow with God's greater glory.[2]

A brief description of these three human dimensions will provide a helpful backdrop for the treatment of the discernment rules. First, the level of external behavior is obvious and practical. External behavior is what you do in the sight of other people. Because this activity is easily observed by others, the danger is that they—and you yourself—can identify you with what you do: You *are* what you do! How easily and insidiously this reduction occurs. This reduction, however, always trivializes human and faith identity. Nonetheless, external behavior, when properly situated in the whole human makeup, does play an important role in acting the mature Christian faith, hope, and love that you profess.

Second, the dimension of inner spontaneity houses all those rational and affective experiences that happen to you, often without your willing or causing them. I call this dimension the "skin" of the soul because it is where feelings, emotions, and affectivity scratch and scamper in you. These spontaneous experiences, both rational and affective, are usually unpredictable and unstable. As a result, this level has a fluctuating nature. When this unpredictability is joined to the intensity and passion of feeling, it can pose a fearful threat. Another dangerous reduction hovers over this area: you *are* what you feel. That reduction overplays the skin of the soul by letting your identity settle in there. I do not mean my depiction of this dimension to be predominantly negative and pejorative. My primary concern is to describe this dimension for what it is. Obviously, it also has an important, passionate contribution to make to your human and faith makeup.

Third, the core of the soul is the most profound, personal, and unique part of you. This aspect of you is like a sanctuary, a holy of holies, where God is creatively loving you breath by breath. Here God's creatively immediate love, described in the Foundation (see chapter 3), burns in a vigil of eternal flame. The white-hot center of this eternal flame is a central point of goodness in you and is a gift of God. To disown or deny this core of the soul is to turn any hope for faithfulness into an impossible fantasy and to reduce love to an unpredictable feeling and an object manipulated in self-promoting behavior. Living without your deepest center, thinking mistakenly that the vigil flame has gone out, is a risky venture indeed, fraught with danger, like a ship whose sails flash uncontrollably in the wind around a broken mast.

These distinctions could not have been clearly recognized and enunciated by Ignatius in the sixteenth century, but an awareness of them will help your appreciation and contemporary application of the rules for the discernment of spirits. I will now comment on each rule.[3]

Discernment Rules for the First Week

Ignatius introduces the discernment rules for the first week in note #313 and follows an orderly treatment after that.

> 313.   RULES TO AID US TOWARD
> PERCEIVING AND THEN
> UNDERSTANDING,
> AT LEAST TO SOME EXTENT,
> THE VARIOUS MOTIONS WHICH ARE
> CAUSED
> IN THE SOUL: THE GOOD MOTIONS
> THAT THEY MAY BE RECEIVED,
> AND THE BAD THAT THEY MAY BE
> REJECTED.
> These rules are suitable for the First Week.

The rules in this first section deal with a primitive, early discernment, whereas the rules of the second section speak of a more advanced and sensitive discernment. The words here, "understanding, at least to some extent," contrast with the words that introduce the second section, "with a more probing discernment of spirits." Prenote #9 refers to gross and open temptations, which are treated in these rules of the first section. Prenote #10, describing someone's temptation under the appearance of good, delineates the situation dealt with in the rules of the second section.

This introduction to discernment presents a simple process of three steps for discerning spontaneous inner spirits. The first step, perceiving (*sentir* in Spanish), is a matter of honest awareness and acknowledgment of the particular spontaneous inner movement. Obviously, without this a process of discerning in faith cannot even begin: you cannot discern what you are not aware of. Nonetheless, we all have devices and deceptions that prevent us from facing up to the reality quietly rumbling in our consciousness. To step beyond these devices of avoidance and projection requires an initial courage and a desire to grow in God's love.

The second step, understanding (*conocer* in Spanish), requires insight and the wisdom of the paschal mystery to interpret the present spontaneous inner experience. Though this step in the process presumes a basic honest perception, it goes beyond that initial courage and enters a whole different realm: an interpretation in faith. Generosity, courage, and sincerity are surpassed here by the ability to see in faith whether this spontaneity is from and leads to God or, rather, leads to greater self-centeredness. This faith vision does not automatically accompany human maturity and therefore cannot be presumed as present in everyone. Nonetheless, it is a gift offered, and must be received, as part of all mature faith.

This ability to see in faith is a share in Jesus' own vision of reality. It is not identical with the "common sense" of our contemporary secular society, nor is it a more civilized version of the pleasure/pain principle branded in the flesh of all humans. A life built on pleasure seeking and pain avoidance, however naturally understandable, is devoid of sacrifice and serious suffering. Self becomes the measure of value for everything, whatever religious terminology may be mistakenly used in justification. A life laid out on the paradigm of Jesus' suffering and death into resurrection is neither all pain nor all pleasure. The focus of such a life is beyond self and on God, and is therefore able to find God's love in both pleasure and pain as exemplified in Jesus' life.

It was the love of his Beloved that led him through the suffering of his passion. It was also the love of his Beloved that led him to the pleasurable time in Bethany with those wonderful friends Martha, Mary, and Lazarus. Growth in this ability to find God in both pleasure and pain involves a freedom from your own natural prejudices, a freedom that only love can bestow. God's love experienced before Jesus on the cross at the end of the First Week anchors this freedom in the Foundation and transcends any pleasure/pain prejudice.

The third step is a matter of applying tactics in faith to the various spontaneous inner movements. These tactics involve actions whereby you do what is right for greater intimacy with God: follow the good, holy movement and stand against the evil, demonic one. These tactical actions get their direction and motivational power from the interpretative vision of the previous step. To interpret that God's love is inviting you to the present sacrifice provides the courage to enter and even welcome, at times even enthusiastically, the suffering of the moment. This third step looks for the courage to act in a way that will integrate it with the faith interpretation.

This simple process of three steps coalesces over time into a daily life of discernment, which must finally be rooted in the core of your soul. Otherwise, such living will not be trustworthy or lasting but will depend too much on the whims of mood and the intensity of the moment. For the beginner, following these three steps formalizes the practice of discernment of spirits and over time imprints it in the heart of daily living. This is the process Ignatius is presuming all through these rules.

> 314. *The First Rule.* In the case of persons who are going from one mortal sin to another, the enemy ordinarily proposes to them apparent pleasures. He makes them imagine delights and pleasure of the senses, in order to hold them fast and plunge them deeper into their sins and vices.

But with persons of this type the good spirit
uses a contrary procedure. Through their good
judgment on problems of morality he stings their
consciences with remorse.

Having laid out the basic process of discernment, Ignatius now
gives examples of how the good and evil spirits move in two very
different persons. The approach of the two fundamentally different
spirits differs according to the spiritual orientation of the person
involved. The person described in this rule is someone unreflective
and spiritually primitive without a determined orientation toward
God. As a result, this person is unconverted and blithely sailing
along with the compass unwittingly set on self. Rather than intentionally sinning mortally, this individual is influenced by the seven
capital impulses to sin which are part of all human interiority.[4]

These impulses are not juridical sins in themselves but are
propensities to sin and have as their goal the protection and pro-
motion of self. Before the wake-up call of serious reflection, this
person is clearly moving in the wrong direction. In a way the most
dangerous aspect of this person is the insensitivity of a complacent
lack of reflection. It is the classic case of being blinded by one's
own glory and thus not able to see what is really happening.

Good and evil spirits, because of their fundamentally different
orientations, have opposing strategies with this person. The evil,
dark spirit, eager to keep the person fixated on self, avoids anything like a wake-up call by presenting imaginary, sensual pleasures
to tighten the fixation. The good, holy spirit, eager for the person
to wake up, sounds a piercing call in healthy guilt and remorse as
this individual begins to take a second look at what is really happening in daily life.

315. *The Second.* In the case of persons who are earnestly purging away their sins, and who are progressing from good to better in the service of God our Lord, the procedure used is the opposite of that described in the First Rule. For in this case it is characteristic of the evil spirit to cause gnawing anxiety, to sadden, and to set up obstacles. In this way he unsettles these persons by false reasons aimed at preventing their progress.

But with persons of this type it is characteristic of the good spirit to stir up courage and strength, consolations, tears, inspirations, and tranquility. He makes things easier and eliminates all obstacles, so that the persons may move forward in doing good.

The person presented here is one of serious spiritual identity, just the opposite of the individual in the previous rule. This person is awakened and turned away from sinful, selfish ways and toward God in loving service of others. Once again the two spirits compete for the person's full energy and identity. The evil spirit, always inimical to the true fulfillment of our humanity, proposes worry, anxiety, doubt, and distrust, hoping to slacken this person's progress.

In the life of Ignatius after his conversion and general confession, in the consoling early stage at Manresa, a thought troubled him concerning his hard schedule of penance and prayer. It was like a voice saying, "How can you stand a life like this for the seventy years you have yet to live?"[5] This gross and open temptation set off the smoke bomb of doubt, confusing and interrupting the progress he was making. It is a good example of the evil spirit's tactic described in this rule.

Acting in a whole different rationale, the good, holy spirit gives courage, strength, peace, and inspiration to continue the progress of a serious spiritual approach, whatever comes in the future. These two rules give you a feel for the reality and orientation of the good and evil spirits by illustrating their different approaches with two different types of people. As Ignatius continues his treatment in the rest of these rules, he is concerned with the spiritually serious person because, as mentioned earlier, the primitive unreflective person has not yet begun a real spiritual life.

> 316. *The Third,* about spiritual consolation. By [this kind of] consolation I mean that which occurs when some interior motion is caused within the soul through which it comes to be inflamed with love of its Creator and Lord. As a result it can love no created thing on the face of the earth in itself, but only in the Creator of them all.
>
> Similarly, this consolation is experienced when the soul sheds tears which move it to love for its Lord—whether they are tears of grief for its own sins, or about the Passion of Christ our Lord, or about other matters directly ordered to his service and praise.
>
> Finally, under the word consolation I include every increase in hope, faith, and charity, and every interior joy which calls and attracts one toward heavenly things and to the salvation of one's soul, by bringing it tranquillity and peace in its Creator and Lord.

After presenting the basic orientations of the two spirits in the spontaneity of your consciousness, Ignatius focuses in the third rule on consolation and in the fourth on desolation. These are the two different interpretations in faith without which we are helpless in the face of various spontaneous inner experiences. Consolation and desolation serve as important lights for interpreting and acting in a serious spiritual life. These spontaneous inner experiences are actual psychic realities in your daily life and, when interpreted in faith, embody God's personal love, always inviting and awaiting your response. They are the warp and woof in you of holiness: that work of art God eagerly desires for you.

Ignatius does not give a snappy, simple definition of consolation. Since it is an inner psychic experience, he gives what might be called a phenomenological description: a variety of human inner experiences, each of which in its own way exemplifies the reality of consolation. Though it registers in you as a psychic reality, consolation always involves an interpretation in faith. In this way consolation is not simply a dictionary term for Ignatius; it is a spiritual reality with relationship in faith to God's love. In his *Autobiography*, he speaks of the great consolation he received during his convalescence in Loyola from looking at the stars. The effect was explicitly spiritual: "When doing so he felt within himself a powerful urge to be serving our Lord."[6] This stirring is different from the professional awe and wonder of an astronomer. Consolation in discernment of spirits is always a spontaneous inner human experience as interpreted spiritually and with spiritual effects.

Spiritual consolation is a spontaneous experience that is moved and stirred in you, but it always invites the ratification of your intentional ownership. In the first sentence of the third rule, the passive constructions "is caused" and "comes to be inflamed" catch the spontaneous nature of spiritual consolation, an experience which leads to the realization that absolutely everything *is*, stands forth in being, because of a loving Creator. So your true self can intentionally love nothing except in relation to such profound love and care.

As the second paragraph of the third rule notes, the inner spontaneity can result in the physiological experience of tears. Here the motive makes all the difference. Tears of self-pity are not consoling, whereas tears motivated by sorrow for sin and Jesus' suffering in the Passion, though uncomfortable, are consoling. In this way the tears are not sad and discouraging but are related to love and mission in response to God.

Consolation is always an increase in faith, hope, and charity, at times without an exciting feeling. A popular misunderstanding is that consolation always "feels good." Sometimes it does feel good, but at other times, as faith deepens into the core beyond the skin of the soul, consolation has no feeling. Yet in some way it is then even more real and dependable. When it invites to an experience that is difficult and painful, as with Jesus in his passion, consolation does not feel nice, easy, or good.

Joy and *peace* are words that are sometimes used too facilely to refer to God's love. Ignatius carefully nuances the joy and peace that characterize consolation. The joy of consolation contains an invitation, a vocation to live in a "heavenly," or Godlike, way by serving others. This heavenly way of living is not utterly removed from this world. Rather, it is living interiorly according to the virtues that are opposite to the seven capital impulses to sin. So the joy of consolation is distinguished from complacency by a zealous fire to share God's love. The peace that characterizes consolation has your Creator and Lord, not yourself, as object. A false peace or idleness, sluggishly nestled in self-concern, is not consolation. Ignatius's phenomenological description of the nuances of consolation is helpful as it sensitizes your reading of your heart and moves from skin-of-soul experience to appropriate behavioral and core results.

> 317. *The Fourth,* about spiritual desolation. By [this kind of] desolation I mean everything which is the contrary of what was described in the Third Rule; for example, obtuseness of soul, turmoil within it, an impulsive motion toward low and earthly things, or disquiet from various agitations and temptations. These move one toward lack of faith and leave one without hope and without love. One is completely listless, tepid, and unhappy, and feels separated from our Creator and Lord.
>
> For just as consolation is contrary to desolation, so the thoughts which arise from consolation are likewise contrary to those which spring from desolation.

Spiritual desolation and consolation are not completely contradictory because they share some spiritual aspects. They are both God-centered, although desolation's version is a God who seems absent. Without some serious appreciation of genuine God-centeredness, the apparent absence of God would not bother you into the disturbance of desolation.[7]

Desolation is never caused by God but is permitted and used by God to teach you important lessons about the spiritual life and holiness. Because of the sinfulness of our human condition, desolation often sprouts in the rich dirt of the skin of the soul. So the desolation of those seven capital impulses cannot be avoided by pulling them out of the garden of your heart, roots and all. Desolation can also sink deeper roots. When this happens, the danger of temptation is more serious, and its detection requires greater enlightenment. The goal of mature spiritual living is never to avoid all desolation—an impossibility—but honestly to recognize it and decisively to deal with it. Ignatius takes desolation very seriously, recognizing its important role in spiritual growth.

Continuing his phenomenological approach, Ignatius uses qualities for desolation that are contrary to those of consolation. An obtuseness or gloominess[8] of soul and impulsive movement to low and earthly things contrast with the lightness and attraction of the heavenly things of consolation. A desolate disquiet and restlessness that contrast with consolation's tranquillity and peace, must be distinguished from a consoling apostolic zeal. The desolate restlessness is stirred by temptations and inner agitations that subtly ferment a sense of distrust of God without much hope and love. Desolation is not usually a loss of intellectual belief in God's providence; rather, as something much more subtle, the temptations tend toward a distrust of God that can take the heart out of hope and love. Apostolic zeal, however, is born in a flaming realization of God's love.

The listlessness, complacency, and boredom of desolation make you feel as though you are separated from your loving Creator. The impulsive mood of desolation plays tricks with your feelings. To feel as if separated from God's love is not equal to actual separation. Because of the subtlety of desolation and because the thoughts and actions that spring from it are contrary to consolation, you must be carefully reflective of your spontaneous interior life, with all its differences, lest it solidify too quickly and mistakenly into an intentional identity, deceptive and discouraging.

The rest of the rules in this first section present tactics to be applied in light of the faith interpretation of either consolation or desolation. As you will see, Ignatius spends more space on the tactics that follow an interpretation of desolation than on those following an interpretation of consolation. Even the two tactics for consolation that he gives are related to dealing with desolation. No formal treatment of spiritual consolation in itself is included in these rules.

> 318. *The Fifth.* During a time of desolation one should never make a change. Instead, one should remain firm and constant in the resolutions and in the decision which one had on the day before the desolation, or in a decision in which one was during a previous time of consolation.
>
> For just as the good spirit is chiefly the one who guides and counsels us in time of consolation, so it is the evil spirit who does this in time of desolation. By following his counsels we can never find the way to a right decision.

This rule presumes the interplay of two experiences: a good decision previously made in a time of consolation and a correct interpretation now of desolation on the skin of your soul. The tactic is not to change the previous good decision. Clear enough—except that the wind of desolate feelings, bearing full brunt on the tiller of your decision, seems at odds with the basic direction of your soul. Such a wind is howling for change and freedom of movement. Genuine insight and courage, the two basic elements of discernment, are needed to stand firm. The principle is stated clearly: in desolation the evil spirit guides and counsels. And following those counsels, you can never find the way to a right decision.

> 319. *The Sixth.* Although we ought not to change our former resolutions in time of desolation, it is very profitable to make vigorous changes in ourselves against the desolation, for example, by insisting more on prayer, meditation, earnest self-examination, and some suitable way of doing penance.

Although you do not change the previous good decision, your goal now is not simply to sit and outwait the stormy blast. Changes are vigorously to be made against the desolation. A vigorous asceticism is engaged, but the object of the asceticism here makes a huge difference. Simply to direct asceticism against yourself is confusing and potentially dangerous; what Ignatius counsels is vigorously to act against the desolation. Simply to act against yourself can destroy or impede the search for your true God-intended self. Whereas to act against your desolate false self is a crucial part of the search for and discovery of your true self eagerly intended and offered by God.

Ignatius gives a list of possible acts of asceticism, each of which flies in the face of the desolate feelings. To insist more on the practical value of prayer in your life, to be more active with your mind in meditating on Gospel texts, to be more than ordinarily reflective about the spontaneous flow of your inner life, to practice some appropriate penance—all of these buttress one another and help to undercut the intensity of your desolate feelings. Besides a renewed conviction about the crucial value of healthy asceticism, we need to experiment with creative contemporary forms that will clip the wings of selfish indulgence and help us to glide freely on the wind of God's loving Spirit.

> 320. *The Seventh.* When we are in desolation we should think that the Lord has left us to our own powers in order to test us, so that we may prove ourselves by resisting the various agitations and temptations of the enemy. For we can do this with God's help, which always remains available, even if we do not clearly perceive it. Indeed, even though the Lord has withdrawn from us his abundant fervor, augmented love, and intensive grace, he still supplies sufficient grace for our eternal salvation.

In these tactics of the first section, Ignatius emphasizes the role of reason and ordered practical thinking. Words like *think, consider, meditate,* and *remember* are sprinkled throughout these rules and highlight the emphasis on reason. God does not give you desolation but teaches you much through your dealing with it. Desolation's disenchanting ring on the skin of your soul, in trying to dissuade you from the direction of your core, unsettles you and invites reflection. The loss of extraordinary fervor and of an intense sense of God's love can leave you empty with an aching fear that, left now on your own, you will not be able to endure. What must be thought about and remembered is that God's love is always present in your core even if it does not seem so. This harks back to the description of desolation (see #317) as the illusory feeling that you are separated from God.

The fervor and grace that have disappeared are extraordinary and special experiences on the skin of your soul. Such consolations are not promised forever; they do fluctuate. But when they are gone, God's love awaits and invites you in the profoundly personal center of your core. A very important truth of revelation must be remembered: sufficient grace is always available for salvation. In this situation God is testing you, although not like a capricious lover. Rather, you are being invited to a depth of love in faith, beyond your imagining yet promised irrefutably in the risen Jesus.

> 321. *The Eighth.* One who is in desolation should strive to preserve himself or herself in patience. This is the counterattack against the vexations which are being experienced. One should remember that after a while the consolation will return again, through the diligent efforts against the desolation which were suggested in the Sixth Rule.

Another ascetic counterattack against the desolation is presented here. In the face of storm winds raging against the sails of your soul, three responses are needed: to strengthen the sails, to batten down the hatches, and to wait in patience for the storm to pass. This patience can seem risky and ill advised, but it makes sense in the light of a bracing act of faith: the consolation of God's love will return. In the meanwhile steps must be taken to protect against the storms of desolation.

Your acts of asceticism against the desolation, mentioned in #319, do not single-handedly cause the return of affective consolation. Rather, they renew your mind and heart in faith to remember and await patiently the promised return of God's love. Without a decisive application of these faith actions, the tidal waters of desolation will wipe out your memory, drown your patience, and swell to a fright that the apparent separation is forever. Desolation, of its nature, when not dealt with decisively tends relentlessly, and

yet subtly, to smuggle you into its own identity. But your identity is
in Jesus, never in desolation: something to think about and always
remember.

> 322. *The Ninth.* There are three chief causes for
> the desolation in which we find ourselves.
>
> The first is that we ourselves are tepid, lazy, or
> negligent in our spiritual exercises. Thus the spiri-
> tual consolation leaves us because of our own
> faults.
>
> The second is that the desolation is meant to
> test how much we are worth and how far we will
> extend ourselves in the service and praise of God,
> even without much repayment by way of consola-
> tions and increased graces.
>
> The third is that the desolation is meant to give us
> a true recognition and understanding, so that we may
> perceive interiorly that we cannot by ourselves bring
> on or retain great devotion, intense love, tears, or any
> other spiritual consolation, but that all these are a gift
> and grace from God our Lord; and further, to prevent
> us from building our nest in a house which belongs to
> Another, by puffing up our minds with pride or vain-
> glory through which we attribute to ourselves the
> devotion or other features of spiritual consolation.

The human mind always wants to understand, so it is natural
for you to think about the causes of desolation. The truth is important enough to bear repetition: God does not cause the desolation
in your heart but permits it for your learning some important

lessons. Desolation is dark and demonic, the work of the evil spirit in your heart—that spirit that Ignatius calls the "enemy of human nature."[9] In the use of this phrase Ignatius presumes, first of all, that human nature is oriented to God but also that a personal evil force is always at work in your heart to subvert that orientation.

Jesus' parable in Matthew 13:24–30 provides valuable background. When questioned about the darnel (a weed), he responds, "Some enemy has done this" (13:28). Yet Jesus is also clear that the darnel and wheat will be allowed to grow together until the end. The mixture of consolation and desolation will continue in all human hearts, which therefore are the only field in which holiness can germinate, bud, and blossom.

The first explanation of desolation centers on you, on the tepidity and laziness that have infected your spiritual practices. The presence of consolation fades into a desolate emptiness because of your own negligence. Your honest awareness of this negligence reflects God's eagerness and invitation that you correct this situation.

The second explanation presents desolation as a means to help you sound ever greater depths in the core of your soul. The intensity of emotional consolations on the skin of your soul is exciting and can motivate much generous activity on your part. But this excitement can also bewitch your heart and shortchange you, depriving your faith commitment of any depth. Without such consolations and inspirations, you will learn how deeply the anchor of your faith has been dropped beneath the beguiling surface waters. Without a felt sense of the Creator's love, to what lengths will you go to live in service and praise of the greater glory of God? This is better learned in the absence of the felt consolation.

The third explanation provides an opportunity to learn some important truths of the spiritual life. You cannot, on your own, cause consolations. As spontaneous experiences on the soul's skin and as a core state, consolation is always a precious gift, promised and given in God's graciousness. In its objective statement, you know this truth. But in the captivating enchantment of consolation, pride can slip in as you think and act like an owner and proprietor. You must live always as one gifted beyond measure and act from your deepest center; desolation appears when we forget these truths.

> 323. *The Tenth.* One who is in consolation should consider how he or she will act in future desolation, and store up new strength for that time.

Though the presumed interpretation in the next two rules is that of consolation, the tactics presented actually apply to desolation. Consolation and desolation have a spontaneous fluctuation built into them; one always follows the other. Despite their inevitable fluctuation, however, no one of the two will fixate forever on the skin of the soul. Deeper in the core, consolation does not fluctuate but is a state of grace that identifies you.

These are truths you are invited to think about as you pray in the midst of experiencing consolation. You are invited to take concrete steps, like writing descriptions in your journal, to remember the consolation when, once again, desolation struts on the stage of your heart.

> 324. *The Eleventh.* One who is in consolation ought to humble and abase herself or himself as much as possible, and reflect how little she or he is

worth in time of desolation when that grace or consolation is absent.

In contrast, one who is in desolation should
reflect that with the sufficient grace already available he or she can do much to resist all hostile
forces, by drawing strength from our Creator and
Lord.

Once again from the midst of the consolation comes an invitation to prayer and serious reflection. Like a surfer on the crest of a
wave of consolation, you need a humble attitude and stance, or the
board will quickly capsize. To force another crest in the curl makes
for sure capsizing. In the curl, velocity from the crest will carry
you. Once again the importance both of the depths of the ocean
beneath the waves and of your core commitment beyond the skin
of your soul cannot be overstated.

325. *The Twelfth.* The enemy conducts himself
like a woman. He is weak when faced by firmness
but strong in the face of acquiescence.

When she is quarreling with a man and he shows
himself bold and unyielding, she characteristically
loses her spirit and goes away. But if the man begins to
lose his spirit and backs away, the woman's anger, vin-
dictiveness, and ferocity swell almost without limit.

In the same way, the enemy characteristically
weakens, loses courage, and flees with his temptations when the person engaged in spiritual endeavors stands bold and unyielding against the enemy's
temptations and goes diametrically against them.

> But if, in contrast, that person begins to fear and
> lose courage in the face of the temptations, there is
> no beast on the face of the earth as fierce as the
> enemy of human nature when he is pursuing his
> damnable intention with his surging malice.

Ignatius's imagination, as mentioned earlier, went through its own transformation as part of his radical conversion of heart to Christ. From self-indulgent fantasizing about romantic chivalry, his imagination was grasped and fascinated by the mystery of Christ. In these last three rules, you have examples of his reoriented imagination in three images that summarize the wisdom of this first section. Unfortunately, the first image is influenced by what we see today as a sexist mentality from his times. If, however, there is any wonder about Ignatius's relationships with women, his many letters would belie any belief that he had a personal prejudice against them.

Nonetheless, the dynamic depicted here, capable obviously of being witnessed in both men and women, repeats a central truth of discernment. Once the desolate wiles of the enemy have been interpreted for what they are, you must decisively apply tactics against the recognized desolation. To waver with indecision and sluggishness will increase the clutches and trap of the desolation. Discernment is no dawdling matter. Rather, it is the decisive lifestyle of someone whose humility is real: attributing the power of defeating the enemy to God as revealed in Jesus, while also exercising a needed resolute cooperative response.

326. *The Thirteenth.* Similarly the enemy acts like
a false lover, insofar as he tries to remain secret and

undetected. For such a scoundrel, speaking with evil intent and trying to seduce the daughter of a good father or the wife of a good husband, wants his words and solicitations to remain secret. But he is deeply displeased when the daughter reveals his deceitful words and evil design to her father, or the wife to her husband. For he easily infers that he cannot succeed in the design he began.

In a similar manner, when the enemy of human nature turns his wiles and persuasions upon an upright person, he intends and desires them to be received and kept in secrecy. But when the person reveals them to his or her good confessor or some other spiritual person who understands the enemy's deceits and malice, he is grievously disappointed. For he quickly sees that he cannot succeed in the malicious project he began, because his manifest deceptions have been detected.

This image comes originally from Ignatius's background of romantic chivalry but exemplifies that transformation of image worked over years and used here in a new way, oriented to the light of Christ. A false lover thrives in secrecy, with deceits and deceptions that require a shadowy, sinister atmosphere. To bring these deceits into the light by revealing them to someone else defuses their insidious spell on your heart.

Once again the heart of the matter is a contemplative humility. This helps you to see what is really happening and to realize that you cannot handle this by yourself in the dark secrecy of your own heart but must risk bringing it into the light. Ignatius is clear about the type of person he is speaking of here. In this rule the individual is called an "upright person," and in the previous rule, a "person engaged in spiritual endeavors." In both instances the person is someone living a serious spiritual life, not the un-awakened, unconverted beginner referred to in #314.

Ignatius is also clear about the type of person to whom the reve-lation is made. Obviously, to open the shadows of your heart to the first person you meet can be dangerous and play unintentionally into the darksome dynamic of the enemy. The revelation is to be made to a "good confessor" or "some other spiritual person who understands the enemy's deceits and malice." In other words the revelation is to be made to someone who appreciates the move-ment of spirits and has the wisdom and courage of discernment. You can imagine the sad, deceptive situation of revealing your "inner secret" to someone who says you are imagining something unreal or, even worse, does not believe in an enemy of human nature.

> 327. *The Fourteenth.* To use still another com-parison, the enemy acts like a military commander who is attempting to conquer and plunder his objective. The captain and leader of an army on campaign sets up his camp, studies the strength and structure of a fortress, and then attacks at its weakest point.
>
> In the same way, the enemy of human nature prowls around and from every side probes all our theological, cardinal, and moral virtues. Then at the point where he finds us weakest and most in need in regard to our eternal salvation, there he attacks and tries to take us.

This time the image comes from Ignatius's military background. A trained military commander surveys the battle scene carefully and plans an attack at the weakest point. The enemy's attack on you is just as intentionally fitted to your central weakness. The heart of a decisive response to the onslaught of the enemy is an honest awareness and active acknowledgment of your cardinal weakness.

Humility, rather than being weak and defenseless, is the powerful counterattack to the enemy. In the secular ideal of strength and self-sufficiency, to have a weakness, much less to acknowledge it as such, is contrary to maturity. But in the warfare of spiritual maturity, humility is the strongest weapon in your arsenal. To acknowledge to yourself, to keep before the eyes of your heart, the area that is your central weakness requires great spiritual strength and the insight of humility.[10] Some people discover that one of the seven capital impulses to sin is their capital weakness, the breeding ground of many subtle insidious temptations. It is the area in which they cannot trust themselves. In fact, sometimes the weakness cuts so deeply that they will never be able to trust themselves in that one area. The mature ideal in this instance is not trusting yourself but in humble honesty living your weakness in a way that entrusts you to God's power and love.

The arrogance of self-sufficiency blunts the alertness of your heart and gives the enemy the upper hand, but humble acknowledgment of your weakness will keep you ready and armed for the enemy's attack. You will know the intimacy of relying completely, not on yourself but on the power of God's love as revealed and promised in Jesus.

Though the discernment described in this treatment of the first set of rules is relatively basic, this more primitive discernment provides an important, courageous commitment and foundation in faith for the further probing discernment described in the next chapter. A lack of experiential appreciation of these dynamics always upends and weakens any further discerning sensitivity.

13

A More Probing Discernment

We begin this chapter with an important caution. Because there are fewer rules than in the first part and my treatment is not as lengthy, this chapter could seem minor and inconsequential. In truth, the case is just the opposite. The rules of this second section aim at a "more probing" discernment of spirits than did those of the first section and require even greater sensitivity on your part. What is needed is not a profusion of words but special insight gained through prayer and holy sensitivity. If you let yourself be drawn into these rules, you will find the Holy Spirit personalizing the wisdom of the tradition contained within them and applying it in a way unique to yourself.

> 328. RULES FOR THE SAME PURPOSE,
> WITH A MORE PROBING
> DISCERNMENT OF SPIRITS.
> These rules are more suitable for the Second
> Week.

These rules build on the previous ones and are aimed at a more sensitive and appreciative sorting out of spontaneous inner spirits.

They are applicable to more advanced temptations, beyond those of the purgative way of the First Week. As the pilgrimage of the spiritual life grows into the illuminative and unitive stages, the temptations are not gross and open but come under the appearance of good.[1] These subtle temptations often relate to the revelation of the Election in the Second Week.

In the First Week the evil ways of the enemy are gross and open. Though at times those ways are not obviously detectable, the critical issue nonetheless is more a matter of courage than of enlightenment. In the rules for the Second Week the evil tactics of the enemy present themselves under the appearance of good. At first glance they seem wise and trustworthy. Ignatius here takes an even more sensitive look at spiritual consolation than in the first set of rules. In fact, the word *desolation* does not occur, because these rules are concerned more with a specially sensitive enlightenment of heart needed to distinguish true from false consolation.

For instance, in his *Autobiography* Ignatius describes two spontaneous inner experiences that appeared to be holy and good but required a more sensitive discernment. In his daily routine at Manresa, which was filled with prayer and penance, the time he had set aside for sleep was being invaded with "great illuminations and spiritual consolation"; these experiences "made him lose much of the time he had set aside for sleep."[2] Later in his life, after his return from the Holy Land, when God's will that he do more study had become clear, he experienced "new light on spiritual things and new delights" that were so strong that he could not do the necessary memorization of Latin grammar.[3] In both these instances, through some prayerful reflection, he realized that these apparently good spontaneous experiences were actually temptations luring him away from following what clearly was God's will for him.

Some examples from our contemporary age also illustrate this issue. Suppose an individual is moved to tears at specific sins each year in retreat but makes no progress in overcoming the sins. The tears (unintentionally) become a release from responsibility to work to correct the sins. Or suppose a talented apostolic person gets ever more active and busy while any significant relationship with Jesus gradually burns out and fizzles into an empty activism. Or, as a third example, a person who had to slow down and relax learns this lesson so well that caring for himself grows into the major venture of that person's life. In each of these cases a spontaneous inner experience that appeared good, wise, and God-given over time is seen to interfere with a person's wholehearted following of God's will of love.

> 329. *The First Rule.* It is characteristic of God and his angels, by the motions they cause, to give genuine happiness and spiritual joy, and thereby to banish any sadness and turmoil induced by the enemy.
>
> It is characteristic of the enemy to fight against this happiness and spiritual consolation, by using specious reasonings, subtleties, and persistent deceits.

This rule basically summarizes what has already been said about the diversity in orientation and in tactics of the good and evil spirits so that it may be applied even more sensitively in the rest of these rules. The genuine nature of spiritual consolation given by God and the good spirit and the specious nature of reasonings against consolation on the part of the enemy constitute the diametrically different orientations of these two agents in your heart: one a protagonist and the other an antagonist. The genuine joy of the good spirit dispels the sadness and turmoil characteristic of desolation induced by the evil spirit. The aim of the evil spirit here, through specious and subtle reasoning and persistent deceit, is to strip the skin of your soul of its genuine joy and peace. The task in these rules is to unmask the fallacious reasoning.

> 330. *The Second.* Only God our Lord can give the soul consolation without a preceding cause. For it is the prerogative of the Creator alone to enter the soul, depart from it, and cause a motion in it which draws the whole person into love of His Divine Majesty. By "without [a preceding] cause" I mean without any previous perception or understanding of some object by means of which the consolation just mentioned might have been stimulated, through the intermediate activity of the person's acts of understanding and willing.

A consolation that carries its own validation cannot be doubted. Ignatius speaks here of a consolation without a preceding cause. This consolation is contrasted with that presented in the next rule, which has a preceding cause. Some distinctions can provide greater clarity about the consolation treated in this rule. The cause referred to is not God, since that divine cause originates both consolations in these two rules; rather, it is some experience of understanding or willing that mediates God's causing of the consolation. Also, this previous mediating cause is not proportionate to the quality of consolation that results.

Another detail is important in Ignatius's description of this special experience. The motion caused here by God "draws the *whole*

person into love of [the] Divine Majesty." An experience of consolation that draws a person totally into love of God is very special
indeed. Ignatius's experience at the Cardoner River in Manresa
seems to fit this description.[4] How frequent such an experience is and
whether degrees are possible in such total absorption into love of
God are questions of much debate. It seems to me that the experience
of being "wholly" drawn into love of God is not susceptible to
degrees. However, there can be degrees of experience of consolation
without previous proportionate cause, and this may not be too rare. It
is clear that Ignatius himself combines all the elements mentioned here
into the description of a consoling experience that is very special.

I append here a wonderful example from Walker Percy, a southern
Catholic novelist and essayist of the last century. The experience
that Percy describes in a letter to Robert Coles at Harvard is an
example of a consolation at Christmas Mass that was surely sur-
prising and not influenced by a previous proportionate cause.
Whether a special consolation draws the whole of a person into
love of the Divine Majesty is hard to measure in any case, and such
a total drawing of Percy is not my claim here. I let Percy speak for
himself:

> The mass was going on, the homily standard—that
> is, "true" but customary. A not-so-good choir of
> young rock musicians got going on "Joy to the
> World," the vocals not so good but enthusiastic.
> Then it hit me: What if it should be the case that
> the entire Cosmos had a creator and what if he
> decided for reasons of his own to show up as a
> little baby, conceived and born under suspicious
> circumstances? Well, Bob, you can lay it to
> Alzheimer's or hangover or whatever, but—it hit

me—I had to pretend I had an allergy attack so I could take out my handkerchief.[5]

331. *The Third.* With or by means of a preceding cause, both the good angel and the evil angel are able to cause consolation in the soul, but for their contrary purposes. The good angel acts for the progress of the soul, that it may grow and rise from what is good to what is better. The evil angel works for the contrary purpose, that is, to entice the soul to his own damnable intention and malice.

Consolation without a previous proportionate cause is so clearly of God that it needs no discernment. That is not the case regarding a consolation with preceding proportionate cause. This type of consolation can be given by the good or the evil spirit. Most commentators would say that consolation given by the good spirit is genuine, whereas consolation given by the evil spirit is apparent and specious. Jules Toner, S.J., however, suggests that the evil spirit can give genuine consolation.[6] Regardless of this difference of opinion, there is total agreement that the two spirits influence the consolation for their diametrically opposed ends. For this reason the rest of the rules present a method and requisite signs for discerning this dramatic yet subtle difference.

332. *The Fourth.* It is characteristic of the evil angel, who takes on the appearance of an angel of light, to enter by going along the same way as the devout soul and then to exit by his own way with success for himself. That is, he brings good and holy thoughts attractive to such an upright soul and then strives

little by little to get his own way, by enticing the soul
over to his own hidden deceits and evil intentions.

When the evil spirit appears to give spiritual consolation, its
approach is that of an angel of light. In this way the evil spirit,
seeming innocuous and appealing at the very beginning, enters the
spiritually serious person's way of thinking and desiring by presenting good and holy thoughts attractive to such a good person.
But gradually these holy thoughts and desires misfire and then
mislead the serious person in a slow shift of focus that makes all the
difference: from God-centered to self-centered.

> *333. The Fifth.* We should pay close attention to
> the whole train of our thoughts. If the beginning,
> middle, and end are all good and tend toward what
> is wholly good, it is a sign of the good angel. But if
> the train of the thoughts which a spirit causes ends
> up in something evil or diverting, or in something
> less good than what the soul was originally propos-
> ing to do; or further, if it weakens, disquiets, or
> disturbs the soul, by robbing it of the peace, tran-
> quillity, and quiet which it enjoyed earlier, all this is
> a clear sign that this is coming from the evil spirit,
> the enemy of our progress and eternal salvation.

This rule and the next two propose three moments, three perspectives for interpreting the specious nature of the evil spirit in
the midst of genuine consolation. The issue here is not simply one
discrete spontaneous inner experience, like a thought, feeling, or
phantasm, but the whole flowing process of a person's spiritual
life. The method proposed here with different moments involves

careful spiritual reflection. Consciousness examen is a prime example of this spiritually reflective method.

This rule focuses on a specific moment in the experience of consolation as influenced by the evil spirit: the end moment of the process. For a movement of consolation to continue as holy, its beginning, middle, and end must be good and God-oriented. When the process concludes in a spirit of disquiet, disturbance, lack of peace, and shrinking generosity, then the touch and presence of the evil spirit have been unmasked. At this point you realize that you have been duped. Much can be learned for the future, but the past cannot be undone. Repentance and wise renewed resolution are the agenda for the future. Though this end-moment recognition in some sense comes too late and should not be the only strategy in your battle plan, sometimes only the clear evidence of the ending allows you to cuff the hand of evil.

> 334. *The Sixth.* When the enemy of human nature has been perceived and recognized by his serpent's tail and the evil end to which he is leading, it then becomes profitable for the person whom he has tempted in this way to examine the whole train of the good thoughts which the evil spirit brought to the soul; that is, how they began, and then how little by little the evil spirit endeavored to bring the soul down from the sweetness and spiritual joy in which it had been, and finally brought it to his own evil intention. The purpose is that through this experience, now recognized and noted, the soul may guard itself in the future against these characteristic snares.

Once you perceive *(sentir)* and recognize *(conocer)* the serpentine poison, then much can be learned by carefully retracing the development of this consolation from the end back to its beginning. In this way you can sort out the good and evil spirits from within the whole developing process. This reminds you that discernment is not like a catechism of questions and answers to be memorized; it is an art that you will always be learning. The art of discernment and holiness will familiarize you over time with patterns of God's love and of demonic selfish love and how they differently mark and stain your lived experience.

> 335. *The Seventh.* In the case of those who are going from good to better, the good angel touches the soul gently, lightly, and sweetly, like a drop of water going into a sponge. The evil spirit touches it sharply, with noise and disturbance, like a drop of water falling onto a stone.
>
> In the case of those who are going from bad to worse, these spirits touch the souls in the opposite manner. The reason for this is the fact that the disposition of the soul is either similar to or different from the respective spirits who are entering. When the soul is different, they enter with perceptible noise and are quickly noticed. When the soul is similar, they enter silently, like those who go into their own house by an open door.

As the art of holiness shapes your sensitivity, you will recognize the touch of the evil spirit earlier in the process of consolation. The spirits make noisy or quiet entrances to your soul. If your life is already seriously in line with the Holy Spirit, the entry of the good spirit is gentle, sweet, and quiet, as though entering a welcoming home with the door wide open, whereas the evil spirit must buck against the flow of your soul, causing upset. This disturbance caused by the evil spirit, however, can at times involve a quiet shiver of spirit, not a deafening thud. A drop of water on a stone is not Niagara Falls! For the unreflective beginner, the entry is just the opposite. God's spirit jolts the person to reflection through the wake-up call of healthy guilt, moving to remorse. However, with this unawakened person the evil spirit quietly, sensuously strengthens the web of infatuation with self.

The three different moments of the process of consolation specified in these three rules form and coalesce into a method of enlightened sensitivity for the two different spirits affecting your daily interior life. When this reflective insight and feel for the spirits is joined to humble courage, a double conflagration occurs: you burn both with an inner fire of intimacy with the risen Jesus and with a growing flame of desire to have that fire shape our universe to ever greater justice and unity.

> 336. *The Eighth.* When the consolation is without a preceding cause there is no deception in it, since it is coming only from God our Lord, as was stated above [330]. However, the spiritual person to whom God gives this consolation ought to examine that experience with great vigilance and attention. One should distinguish the time when the consolation itself was present from the time after it, in which the soul remains still warm and favored with the gifts and aftereffects of the consolation which has itself passed away. For often during this

later period we ourselves act either through our
own reasoning which springs from our own habits
and the conclusions we draw from our own concepts and judgments, or through the influence of
either a good or an evil spirit. In this way we form
various projects and convictions which are not
coming immediately from God our Lord. Hence
these need to be very carefully examined before
they are fully accepted or carried into effect.

This concluding rule is an important footnote to the treatment
of consolation without a previous proportionate cause. As stated
earlier, such an experience is instigated by God alone. But the
afterglow of such special consolation is a different experience and
is separable from it. In that separation a variety of other influences
can intervene. Sometimes very strong desires lead to unreasonable
decisions. These desires and decisions are not self-validating.
They require a cooling-off period of time, patience, and careful
reflection after the heat of the special consolation. Decisions and
projects for follow-up in the afterglow can overstep the evidence
and boundaries of discernment and reason, leading to discouragement, frustration, and even distrust of God in our religious experience. At this point in the experience of the Exercises and of
discernment, these signs are evidence loud and clear of the work of
the wily, evil spirit.

EPILOGUE

Stretched for greater glory: an exciting enterprise! The glory shining on the face of the risen Jesus, sparkling like sun-dazzled snow, is beyond all comparison. The radiance of that sparkle infatuates us in a contemplative absorption beyond our own awareness and reflection. This heart-to-heart encounter with God in the risen Jesus is the core of the Spiritual Exercises. It roots, steadies, balances, and guides the flow of the whole experience. This ongoing encounter stretches our hearts to the limits of the universe and beyond for transformation in a radiance of greater glory meant to nourish and dazzle us all.

But this stretching and being stretched is not all ease and comfort. The dynamics of the Exercises do not jerk us aimlessly this way and that. Nonetheless, being stretched brings painful aches to muscles and tendons atrophied from years of complacency. But even for those people healthily stretched already, the increasing radiance, the movement to glory ever greater, induces pain and suffering. This book's description of the developing dynamics of the Exercises makes that clear. But the ache and anguish in the stretching also promise an exhilaration of spirit in freedom, zealous desire, and compassionate service. It is an exhilaration that excites and confirms even as it stretches.

Sails snapping and cracking in the stretch of spirited winds are much more exciting than sails listlessly drooping. However, sails flashing recklessly in the crosscurrents are dangerous and destructive. The art of sailing always involves an experiential competence that has learned to balance the sails properly in the crosscurrents of the headwinds. Sailing's art is also humbly aware of dependence on the winds. No luck and no brazen insolence can manage this art. Without its art and practiced competence, sailing rushes to danger and destruction. Direction and guidance, not luck, are key. To find a compass for guidance in the glory of sun, moon, stars, planets; to trust, cling to, and follow the North Star of God's exquisite love glittering brightly, faithfully, like a jewel in the morning sky: this is to be stretched for greater glory.

Ignatius found his way through the swirling waves and blustery winds of his heart. As he learned to read the signs properly, an overeager application of self became a wholehearted, watchful readiness for greater glory revealed *de arriba* by the Divine Majesty. Once the greater glory was revealed, his humble freedom always found courage to follow anywhere in God's creation, because he knew he was never, never alone. This greater glory took him, and will continue to take Ignatian followers, to some very unlikely places.

A pilgrim mystic always on the road, aglow with thankfulness in the midst of all the gifts, serves in company with the risen Jesus. That great Faithful Witness is always present, with an intimacy and fidelity beyond imagining, until the final stretching of the Holy Spirit for a greater glory, then dazzlingly ablaze in the eternity of God.

NOTES

Introduction

1. See Javier Melloni, *The Exercises of St. Ignatius Loyola in the Western Tradition* (Herefordshire, England: Gracewing, 2000).

2. See Ignatius of Loyola, *St. Ignatius' Own Story, As Told to Luis González de Cámara; with a Sampling of His Letters*, trans. William J. Young (Chicago: Loyola Press, 1956), chaps. 1–3.

3. See Ignatius of Loyola, *The Spiritual Exercises of Saint Ignatius: A Translation and Commentary*, trans. George E. Ganss (St. Louis: Institute of Jesuit Sources, 1992), pp. 28–29, #20.

4. Ibid., pp. 27–28, #19.

5. *The New Testament in Modern English*, trans. J. B. Phillips (New York: Macmillan, 1958).

6. Two examples of commentaries are Michael Ivens, *Understanding the Spiritual Exercises* (Herefordshire, England: Gracewing, 1998), and Katherine Dyckman, Mary Garvin, and Elizabeth Liebert, *The Spiritual Exercises Reclaimed: Uncovering Liberating Possibilities for Women* (New York: Paulist Press, 2001).

1. Ignatius's Spiritual Exercises and the Word of God

1. Paul Shore, *The "Vita Christi" of Ludolph of Saxony and Its Influence on the Spiritual Exercises of Ignatius of Loyola*, Studies in the Spirituality of Jesuits, vol. 30 (January 1998).

2. Ignatius of Loyola, *St. Ignatius' Own Story, As Told to Luis González de Cámara; with a Sampling of His Letters*, trans. William J. Young (Chicago: Loyola Press, 1956), p. 11, #11.

3. See Gilles Cusson, *Biblical Theology and the Spiritual Exercises: A Method toward a Personal Experience of God As Accomplishing within Us His Plan of Salvation*, trans. Mary Angela Roduit and George E. Ganss (St. Louis: Institute of Jesuit Sources, 1988), pp. 7, 39.

4. See Ibid., pp. 3–6.

5. Ignatius of Loyola, *St. Ignatius' Own Story*, p. 22, #27.

6. John W. O'Malley, *The First Jesuits* (Cambridge: Harvard University Press, 1993), p. 37.

7. Cusson, *Biblical Theology*.

8. Ibid., p. 41.

9. This is also the central approach of Cusson's masterful treatment and is why I rely heavily on his treatment in this book.

10. William A. M. Peters, *The Spiritual Exercises of St. Ignatius: Exposition and Interpretation* (Jersey City: Program to Adapt the Spiritual Exercises, 1968), p. 56.

11. See Ignatius of Loyola, *St. Ignatius' Own Story*, pp. 23–24, #30.

12. See Walter L. Farrell, "The Background of the Spiritual Exercises in the Life of St. Ignatius of Loyola," in *A New Introduction to the Spiritual Exercises of St. Ignatius*, ed. John E. Dister (Collegeville, Minn.: Liturgical Press, 1993), pp. 25–39.

13. Ibid., pp. 27–28.

14. Ignatius of Loyola, *The Spiritual Exercises of Saint Ignatius: A Translation and Commentary*, trans. George E. Ganss (St. Louis: Institute of Jesuit Sources, 1992), pp. 146–47.

15. Cusson, *Biblical Theology*, pp. 85–88.

16. In the introductory prenotes it is clear that the experience is a one-on-one encounter of giving and receiving the Exercises.

2. Preliminary Profound Practicalities

1. See John W. O'Malley, "Some Distinctive Characteristics of Jesuit Spirituality in the Sixteenth Century," in John W. O'Malley, John W. Padberg, and Vincent T. O'Keefe, *Jesuit Spirituality: A Now and Future Resource* (Chicago: Loyola Press, 1990), pp. 1–20.

2. Charles E. O'Neill, *"Acatamiento": Ignatian Reverence in History and in Contemporary Culture*, Studies in the Spirituality of Jesuits, vol. 8 (January 1976): p. 7.

3. See also Ignatius of Loyola, *The Constitutions of the Society of Jesus*, trans. George E. Ganss (St. Louis: Institute of Jesuit Sources, 1970), p. 96, #65.

4. Ignatius of Loyola, *The Spiritual Exercises of Saint Ignatius: A Translation and Commentary*, trans. George E. Ganss (St. Louis: Institute of Jesuit Sources, 1992), p. 144.

5. Ibid., pp. 124–25, #325–327.

6. Ignatius of Loyola, *St. Ignatius' Own Story, As Told to Luis González de Cámara; with a Sampling of His Letters,* trans. William J. Young (Chicago: Loyola Press, 1956), p. 21, #25.

7. See Karl Rahner, *The Dynamic Element in the Church,* trans. W. J. O'Hara (New York: Herder and Herder, 1964), pp. 93–94. In the note here, Rahner wonders whether Ignatius at first had "the look of an [Illuminist]" and so Ignatius added details to the *Exercises* to prevent that early misunderstanding.

8. See Ignatius of Loyola, *Spiritual Exercises,* p. 125, #326.

9. See Joseph A. Tetlow, "Lightworks," in *Choosing Christ in the World: Directing the Spiritual Exercises of St. Ignatius Loyola According to Annotations Eighteen and Nineteen: A Handbook* (St. Louis: Institute of Jesuit Sources, 1989), pp. 257–95.

10. See O'Malley, "Distinctive Characteristics," in O'Malley, Padberg, and O'Keefe, *Jesuit Spirituality,* p. 19.

3. A Glorious Foundation

1. See Ignatius of Loyola, *The Spiritual Exercises of Saint Ignatius: A Translation and Commentary,* trans. George E. Ganss (St. Louis: Institute of Jesuit Sources, 1992), p. 48, #75.

2. See William A. M. Peters, *The Spiritual Exercises of St. Ignatius: Exposition and Interpretation* (Jersey City: Program to Adapt the Spiritual Exercises, 1968), pp. 23–24.

3. Ignatius of Loyola, *The Spiritual Exercises of Saint Ignatius: A Translation and Commentary,* trans. George E. Ganss (St. Louis: Institute of Jesuit Sources, 1992), p. 32, #23.

4. Joseph A. Tetlow, *The Fundamentum: Creation in the Principle and Foundation,* Studies in the Spirituality of Jesuits, vol. 21 (September 1989): p. 2.

5. Ignatius of Loyola, *Spiritual Exercises,* p. 32, #23.

6. Ibid., throughout but especially p. 20. Tetlow has documented this existential and experiential view of the Creator/creature relationship as the one Ignatius and the early Jesuits practiced as narrated in the sixteenth-century Directories about the *Exercises.* In fact, the Latin word *fundamentum* is always used (also by Tetlow) to denote something different from "the philosophical plan of God" approach of the Principle and Foundation. In

the Exercises the director is urged not simply to give *(dar* in Spanish) but to explain and talk through *(platicar)* this foundation. This view of the present immediacy of creation is so important that talking it over with the retreatant is urged even though this seems a momentary violation of the brief comments to which prenote #2 invites the director.

7. In using the English word *foundation* in my description here, I intend Tetlow's version of Ignatius's original view.

8. Gilles Cusson, *Biblical Theology and the Spiritual Exercises: A Method toward a Personal Experience of God As Accomplishing within Us His Plan of Salvation,* trans. Mary Roduit and George E. Ganss (St. Louis: Institute of Jesuit Sources, 1988), p. 53.

9. Ignatius of Loyola, *Spiritual Exercises,* p. 32, #23.

10. Tetlow, *Fundamentum,* p. 42.

11. Ignatius of Loyola, *Spiritual Exercises,* p. 32, #23.

12. See Cusson, *Biblical Theology,* pp. 77–79.

4. A Forgiven Sinner: Awed in Gratitude

1. Gilles Cusson, *Biblical Theology and the Spiritual Exercises: A Method toward a Personal Experience of God As Accomplishing within Us His Plan of Salvation,* trans. Mary Roduit and George E. Ganss (St. Louis: Institute of Jesuit Sources, 1988), pp. 157–62.

2. Ibid., p. 161.

3. Winoc De Broucker, *The First Week of the Exercises* (Jersey City: Program to Adapt the Spiritual Exercises, January 1959 in *Christus* magazine 21), p. 8.

4. *The New Testament in Modern English,* trans. J. B. Phillips (New York: Macmillan, 1958).

5. Michael Ivens, "The First Week: Some Notes on the Text," *Way Supplement* 48 (autumn 1983): p. 7.

6. Cusson, *Biblical Theology,* p. 137.

7. Ignatius of Loyola, *The Spiritual Exercises of Saint Ignatius: A Translation and Commentary,* trans. George E. Ganss (St. Louis: Institute of Jesuit Sources, 1992), pp. 40–41, #48; p. 43, #55.

8. Ibid., p. 45, #63.

9. Michael Ivens, *Understanding the Spiritual Exercises* (Herefordshire, England: Gracewing, 1998), pp. 69–70.

10. George A. Aschenbrenner, *Quickening the Fire in Our Midst: The Challenge of Diocesan Priestly Spirituality* (Chicago: Loyola Press, 2002), p. 106.

11. See John W. O'Malley's essay "Some Distinctive Characteristics of Jesuit Spirituality in the Sixteenth Century," in John W. O'Malley, John W. Padberg, and Vincent T. O'Keefe, *Jesuit Spirituality: A Now and Future Resource* (Chicago: Loyola Press, 1990), p. 5.

5. Readied for Wise Loving

1. See Gilles Cusson, *Biblical Theology and the Spiritual Exercises: A Method toward a Personal Experience of God As Accomplishing within Us His Plan of Salvation,* trans. Mary Roduit and George E. Ganss (St. Louis: Institute of Jesuit Sources, 1988), pp. 188–89.

2. Ignatius of Loyola, *The Spiritual Exercises of Saint Ignatius: A Translation and Commentary,* trans. George E. Ganss (St. Louis: Institute of Jesuit Sources, 1992), p. 42, #53.

3. See Keith Clark, *Being Sexual—and Celibate* (Notre Dame, Ind.: Ave Maria Press, 1986), p. 41.

4. The title Divine Majesty for God occurs most frequently in the special Ignatian meditations and the election material of the second week. *Divine Majesty* reverberates with a wholehearted, carefully nuanced generosity of reverent loving in loyalty to the beloved. The ideal of sixteenth-century chivalry is radiant with that spirit. The Election, as the following chapters will make clear, is an expression of such loyalty carefully discerned, awaited, and then enthusiastically received *de arriba* ("from above") in the revelation of the beloved Divine Majesty.

5. See Hugo Rahner, *Ignatius the Theologian,* trans. Michael Barry (New York: Herder and Herder, 1968), pp. 3–10.

6. See Karl Rahner, "Ignatian Mysticism of Joy in the World," in *Theological Investigations,* trans. Cornelius Ernst, vol. 3 (Baltimore: Helicon Press, 1967), p. 291.

7. Ignatius of Loyola, *Spiritual Exercises,* p. 53, #91.

8. Ibid., pp. 54–55, #94–98.

9. Ibid., p. 55, #98.

6. A School of Discipleship

1. Ignatius of Loyola, *The Spiritual Exercises of Saint Ignatius: A Translation and Commentary,* trans. George E. Ganss (St. Louis: Institute of Jesuit Sources, 1992), pp. 126–28, #328–336.

2. Ignatius of Loyola, *St. Ignatius' Own Story, As Told to Luis González de Cámara; with a Sampling of His Letters,* trans. William J. Young (Chicago: Loyola Press, 1956), p. 22, #27.

3. Catholic Church, "Dogmatic Constitution on the Church in the Modern World," in *The Documents of Vatican II* (New York: Guild Press, 1966).

4. This description is ascribed by a number of people to William McNamara, O.C.D., though I could not find it in any of his works.

5. George A. Aschenbrenner, "Becoming Whom We Contemplate," *Way Supplement* 52 (spring 1985): p. 32.

6. Luke Timothy Johnson, *Living Jesus: Learning the Heart of the Gospel* (San Francisco: HarperSanFrancisco, 1999), chap. 4.

7. Ignatius of Loyola, *Spiritual Exercises,* p. 56, #104.

8. See David M. Stanley, "Contemplation of the Gospels, Ignatius Loyola, and the Contemporary Christian," *Theological Studies* 29 (September 1968): pp. 417–43.

9. See Karl Rahner, *Spiritual Exercises,* trans. Kenneth Baker (New York: Herder and Herder, 1965), p. 136.

10. Ignatius of Loyola, *Spiritual Exercises,* p. 58, #114; p. 59, #116.

11. Karl Rahner, *Spiritual Exercises,* pp. 114–15.

12. Ignatius of Loyola, *Spiritual Exercises,* p. 62, #130.

13. See Hugo Rahner, *Ignatius the Theologian,* trans. Michael Barry (New York: Herder and Herder, 1968), pp. 181–213.

7. A Cosmic Confrontation

1. Robert Barron, *And Now I See . . . : A Theology of Transformation* (New York: Crossroad, 1998), p. 4.

2. See Ignatius of Loyola, *The Spiritual Exercises of Saint Ignatius: A Translation and Commentary,* trans. George E. Ganss (St. Louis: Institute of Jesuit Sources, 1992), pp. 124–25, #325–327.

3. Ibid., p. 65, #140.

4. Ibid., p. 66, #142.

5. Louis Evely, *A Religion for Our Time,* trans. Brian Thompson and Marie-Claude Thompson (New York: Herder and Herder, 1968), p. 57.

6. See Ignatius of Loyola, *Spiritual Exercises,* pp. 42–43, #54.

7. Ibid., p. 69, #156.

8. Choosing and Loving Always for God's Glory

1. Ignatius of Loyola, *The Spiritual Exercises of Saint Ignatius: A Translation and Commentary,* trans. George E. Ganss (St. Louis: Institute of Jesuit Sources, 1992), p. 68, #152.

2. Michael J. Buckley, *Mission in Companionship: Of Jesuit Community and Communion,* Studies in the Spirituality of Jesuits, vol. 11 (September 1979): pp. 3–4.

3. Ibid., pp. 4–5.

4. Ignatius of Loyola, *Spiritual Exercises,* p. 68, #151.

5. David L. Fleming, *Draw Me into Your Friendship: A Literal Translation and a Contemporary Reading of The Spiritual Exercises* (St. Louis: Institute of Jesuit Sources, 1996), p. 117.

6. Ibid., p. 119.

7. See Gerald G. May, *Addiction and Grace* (San Francisco: Harper and Row, 1988).

8. Ignatius of Loyola, *Spiritual Exercises,* p. 72, #164.

9. Ibid., pp. 72–73, #167.

10. Francis of Assisi, "True and Perfect Joy," in *Francis and Clare: The Complete Works,* trans. Regis J. Armstrong and Ignatius C. Brady (New York: Paulist Press, 1982), pp. 165–66.

11. Karl Rahner, *Spiritual Exercises,* trans. Kenneth Baker (New York: Herder and Herder, 1965), p. 202.

12. For a full professional treatment of the election in the *Exercises,* see Jules J. Toner, *Discerning God's Will: Ignatius of Loyola's Teaching on Christian Decision Making* (St. Louis: Institute of Jesuit Sources, 1991).

13. Ignatius presumed the possibility of permanent commitment. So do I. I do not argue this possibility. Our postmodern culture has lost much of this belief and its resulting stability in a culture. I hope we do not stunt our human potential by denying this possibility.

14. See Karl Rahner, *The Dynamic Element in the Church*, trans. W. J. O'Hara (New York: Herder and Herder, 1964), p. 94.

9. A Compassionate Joy beyond Any Disappointment

1. Ignatius of Loyola, *The Spiritual Exercises*, #193. I am using a combination of two translations that have slight differences on this point: *The Spiritual Exercises of Saint Ignatius: A Translation and Commentary*, trans. George E. Ganss (St. Louis: Institute of Jesuit Sources, 1992), and *The Spiritual Exercises of St. Ignatius*, trans. Louis Puhl (Chicago: Loyola Press, 1951).

2. Ignatius of Loyola, *Spiritual Exercises*, trans. Ganss, p. 83, #203.

3. Ibid., p. 82, #196.

4. Ibid., p. 91, #221.

5. Ibid.

6. Ibid., p. 91, #223.

7. See Gilles Cusson, *Biblical Theology and the Spiritual Exercises: A Method toward a Personal Experience of God As Accomplishing within Us His Plan of Salvation*, trans. Mary Roduit and George E. Ganss (St. Louis: Institute of Jesuit Sources, 1988), pp. 304–307.

8. Ignatius of Loyola, *Spiritual Exercises*, trans. Ganss, p. 92, #224. In #316 Ignatius describes consolation. I will treat this in chapter 12.

9. This is the practice of consciousness examen, which I wrote about in "Consciousness Examen," *Review for Religious* 21 (January 1972): pp. 14–21; "A Check on Our Availability: The Examen," Ibid. 39 (May 1980): pp. 321–24; and "Consciousness Examen: Becoming God's Heart for the World," Ibid. 47 (December 1988): pp. 801–10.

10. Daily Life: Gratefully Serving God in All

1. Ignatius of Loyola, *The Spiritual Journal of St. Ignatius Loyola*, trans. William J. Young (Woodstock, Md.: Woodstock College Press, 1958).

2. Karl Rahner, "Ignatian Mysticism of Joy in the World," in *Theological Investigations*, trans. Cornelius Ernst, vol. 3 (Baltimore: Helicon Press, 1967), p. 280.

3. James Brodrick, *The Origin of the Jesuits* (Westport, Conn.: Greenwood Press, 1971), pp. 16–17.

4. Ignatius of Loyola, *The Spiritual Exercises of Saint Ignatius: A Translation and Commentary*, trans. George E. Ganss (St. Louis: Institute of Jesuit Sources, 1992), p. 94, #230-31.

5. Ibid., p. 80, #189

6. Ibid., p. 94, #232.

7. Ibid., p. 40, #47.

8. Ibid., p. 56, #102.

9. Michael Buckley, "The Contemplation to Attain Love," *Way Supplement* 24 (spring 1975): pp. 92-104.

10. Ibid., p. 100.

11. Ignatius of Loyola, *Spiritual Exercises*, pp. 234-35, #234.

12. Buckley, "Contemplation," p. 101.

13. Ignatius of Loyola, *Spiritual Exercises*, p. 95, #234.

14. Ibid., p. 95, #235.

15. Buckley, "Contemplation," p. 101.

16. Ibid., p. 102.

17. Ignatius of Loyola, *Spiritual Exercises*, p. 95, #236.

18. Buckley, "Contemplation," p. 102.

19. Ibid.

20. Ibid.

21. Ibid.

22. Ignatius of Loyola, *Spiritual Exercises*, p. 95, #237.

23. Buckley, "Contemplation," p. 103.

24. Ibid., p. 104.

25. See "Consciousness Examen," *Review for Religious* 21 (January 1972): pp. 14-21; "A Check on Our Availability: The Examen," Ibid. 39 (May 1980): pp. 321-24; and "Consciousness Examen: Becoming God's Heart for the World," Ibid. 47 (December 1988): pp. 801-10.

11. Methods of Praying and Some Rules

1. John W. O'Malley, *The First Jesuits* (Cambridge: Harvard University Press, 1993), p. 41.

2. Ignatius of Loyola, *St. Ignatius' Own Story, As Told to Luis González de Cámara; with a Sampling of His Letters,* trans. William J. Young (Chicago: Loyola Press, 1956), pp. 19–21, #22–25.

3. Michael Ivens, *Understanding the Spiritual Exercises* (Herefordshire, England: Gracewing, 1998), p. 238.

4. Ignatius of Loyola, *The Spiritual Exercises of Saint Ignatius: A Translation and Commentary,* trans. George E. Ganss (St. Louis: Institute of Jesuit Sources, 1992), pp. 49–50, #82–83.

5. Ibid., p. 88, #213.

6. See Thomas E. Clarke, "Jesus at Table: The Ignatian Rules and Human Hunger Today," in *Ignatian Spirituality in a Secular Age,* ed. George P. Schner (Waterloo, Canada: Wilfrid Laurier University Press, 1984).

7. O'Malley, *First Jesuits,* p. 50.

8. Ivens, *Spiritual Exercises,* p. 250.

9. Michael Buckley, "Ecclesial Mysticism in the Spiritual Exercises: Two Notes on Ignatius, the Church, and Life in the Spirit" (paper presented at the Congreso Internacional de Ejercicios, Loyola, Spain, September 1991), p. 29.

10. Ivens, *Spiritual Exercises,* p. 248.

11. Ignatius of Loyola, *Spiritual Exercises,* p. 133, #353; p. 135, #365.

12. See Buckley, "Ecclesial Mysticism," pp. 25–26, where he argues for a mysticism of union underlying the mysticism of service.

13. Ibid., p. 29.

14. Ignatius of Loyola, *Spiritual Exercises,* p. 135, #365.

15. Buckley, "Ecclesial Mysticism," p. 30.

12. Discernment of Spirits in the Exercises

1. See George A. Aschenbrenner, *Quickening the Fire in Our Midst: The Challenge of Diocesan Priestly Spirituality* (Chicago: Loyola Press, 2002), chap. 9.

2. See George A. Aschenbrenner, "A Hidden Self Grown Strong," in *Handbook of Spirituality for Ministers,* ed. Robert J. Wicks (New York: Paulist Press, 1995), pp. 228–48.

3. See Jules J. Toner, *A Commentary on Saint Ignatius' Rules for the Discernment of Spirits: A Guide to the Principles and Practice* (St. Louis: Institute of Jesuit Sources, 1982). Toner's expert study was very helpful for my own reflections here.

4. William A. M. Peters, *The Spiritual Exercises of St. Ignatius: Exposition and Interpretation* (Jersey City: Program to Adapt the Spiritual Exercises, 1968), p. 190.

5. Ignatius of Loyola, *St. Ignatius' Own Story, As Told to Luis González de Cámara; with a Sampling of His Letters,* trans. William J. Young (Chicago: Loyola Press, 1956), pp. 17–18, #20.

6. Ibid., pp. 11–12, #11.

7. Toner, *Commentary,* pp. 125–26, 138–39.

8. Ibid., p. 127.

9. Ignatius of Loyola, *The Spiritual Exercises of Saint Ignatius: A Translation and Commentary,* trans. George E. Ganss (St. Louis: Institute of Jesuit Sources, 1992), pp. 124–25, #325–27.

10. Consciousness examen plays an important role in this regular acknowledgment.

13. A More Probing Discernment

1. Ignatius of Loyola, *The Spiritual Exercises of Saint Ignatius: A Translation and Commentary,* trans. George E. Ganss (St. Louis: Institute of Jesuit Sources, 1992), p. 24, #10.

2. Ignatius of Loyola, *St. Ignatius' Own Story, As Told to Luis González de Cámara; with a Sampling of His Letters,* trans. William J. Young (Chicago: Loyola Press, 1956), p. 21, #26.

3. Ibid., pp. 39–40, #54–55.

4. Ibid., pp. 23–24, #30.

5. Jay Tolson, *Pilgrim in the Ruins: A Life of Walker Percy* (New York: Simon and Schuster, 1992), pp. 466–67.

6. Jules J. Toner, *A Commentary on Saint Ignatius' Rules for the Discernment of Spirits: A Guide to the Principles and Practice* (St. Louis: Institute of Jesuit Sources, 1982), pp. 228–31.